Networks, Infrastructure, and the New Task for Regulation

Edited by
Werner Sichel and Donald L. Alexander

Ann Arbor
THE UNIVERSITY OF MICHIGAN PRESS

Copyright © by the University of Michigan 1996
All rights reserved
Published in the United States of America by
The University of Michigan Press
Manufactured in the United States of America
⊗ Printed on acid-free paper

1999   1998   1997   1996   4   3   2   1

A CIP catalog record for this book is available from the British Library.

Library of Congress Cataloging-in-Publication Data

Networks, infrastructure, and the new task for regulation / edited by
  Werner Sichel and Donald L. Alexander.
      p.   cm.
  Includes bibliographical references.
  ISBN 0-472-10687-2 (hardcover : alk. paper)
  1. Telecommunication policy—United States.   2. Public utilities—
Government policy—United States.   3. Computer networks—Government
policy—United States.   I. Sichel, Werner.   II. Alexander, Donald
L., 1956–
HE7781.N486   1996
384'.068—dc20   95-42233
                                                                 CIP

Contents

Introduction

Werner Sichel and Donald L. Alexander

Network systems provide significant benefits to both buyers and sellers and are an integral part of the structure of many contemporary industries. In the telecommunication sector, for example, networks allow users to enjoy the benefits of communicating with a wide range of other users that would be prohibitively costly if each user had to rely on making a direct connection with other users. In the airline industry, carriers are able to aggregate traffic through a hub-and-spoke system that allows them to provide their services at a low unit cost that results from a higher degree of resource utilization. And in a similar fashion, firms in the electric power industry employ networks to facilitate the distribution of power across different regions of the country, making it less likely that "brownouts" will occur from unanticipated surges in demand. Indeed, the emergence of local area networks in many business offices has likely improved the efficiency of business communications. Thus, it is accurate to say that networks have had a positive impact on the way that resources are allocated in many sectors of the economy.

Notwithstanding the significant benefits that networks offer, there is concern that the presence of a network may also have an adverse effect on competition and resource allocation within an industry. It was AT&T's former control of the local and long-distance telecommunications network that was cited in the *Modified Final Judgment* as a major reason for AT&T's exercise of market power and also as a rationale for the divestiture of AT&T into a long-distance company separate from the seven independent regional Bell operating companies.[1] More recently, the consolidation of several airlines combined with the growing trend toward greater concentration at hub-dominated airports has raised

---

1. See Robert W. Crandall, "The Role of the U.S. Local Operating Companies," in *Changing the Rules: Technological Change, International Competition, and Regulation in Communications,* ed. Robert W. Crandall and Kenneth Flamm (Washington, D.C.: Brookings Institution, 1989).

questions concerning the competitiveness of prices at these airports.[2] In the electric power industry, legislators have mandated open access to the transmission network to insure that nonintegrated utilities are able to transmit power without fear of being foreclosed from the marketplace.[3] In all three of these examples, the industry had recently been partially or completely deregulated. This raises several important questions regarding the interrelationships among networks, competition, technological change, and optimal regulatory policy. First, is competition likely to thrive in industries in which networks are fundamentally important to the provision of the services? Second, if an industry is at least partially deregulated to promote competition, can the residual regulations be designed so as to provide the proper incentives for efficient use of the network and, perhaps more importantly, so as to encourage the socially optimal amount of investment in network capacity? And third, will networks continue to emerge, independent of specific regulatory changes, as a function of technological advances? These questions and others raise new and interesting research topics for economists to consider. Simultaneously, the proliferation of networks combined with rapid technological change in these industries present legislators and regulators with immediate and difficult choices about how best to shape the regulatory structure, process, and policy toward relying on competitive market forces to "regulate" these industries.

The Tenth Michigan Conference on Public Utility Economics, Networks, Infrastructure and the New Task for Regulation, held over a two-day period at Western Michigan University in 1993, afforded a good and timely opportunity to discuss the aforementioned questions. The Inter-University Committee on Public Utility Economics, supported by a grant from Michigan Bell (Ameritech), brought together prominent academic economists, regulators, and legislators to discuss the major economic issues regarding network services, to summarize the research findings to date, and to consider possible solutions to the complex policy questions that are important to regulators and legislators. Although no single issue was resolved and no specific policy proposal was accepted or rejected, the exchange of ideas and lively debate among the participants served to sharpen the focus on the critical questions that are likely to

2. See GAO, "Airline Competition: Higher Fares and Reduced Competition at Concentrated Airports," Report to Congressional Requesters (Washington, D.C.: GPO, July 1990); and Severin Borenstein, "Hubs and High Fares: Dominance and Market Power in the U.S. Airline Industry," *Rand Journal of Economics* 20 (Autumn 1989): 344–65.

3. See Richard J. Gilbert, Edward Kahn, and Matthew White, "The Efficiency of Market Coordination: Evidence from Wholesale Electric Power Pools," in this volume.

shape the future as we move into the twenty-first century. This volume is separated into three parts, each composed of an introduction and two essays. This parallels the nine presentations made at the conference.

In his insightful introduction to the essays contained in part 1, Professor Kenneth D. Boyer discusses the externalities associated with the provision of network services and contrasts this situation with the traditional externality problem in which one person's action affects a second person's welfare. He notes that the major difference is that buyers and sellers are connected directly and indirectly through many paths in a network system and that changes in one path could potentially affect a wide range of other network users and service providers. For example, the decision to expand capacity at one hub airport decreases unit costs at that airport because of improved traffic flow, but potentially increases unit costs at some other airport(s) because of the reduction in traffic. The simple analysis of expanding capacity to alleviate congestion along one particular path in a network system becomes complicated because it will affect the supply and demand conditions for a wide range of users and providers differently. Consequently, given the far-reaching impact of investment decisions made in network systems, regulators are obliged to consider complex trade-offs in the regulatory process.

Boyer suggests that the "bypass problem," which is of paramount importance in the telecommunication industry, is another example of the externality problem that arises in a network system because of the subsequent reduction in the number of direct and indirect connections. As users leave the system, this reduces the benefits to the users who remain connected to the system. An individual has a greater incentive to leave the system, ceteris paribus, since there is a divergence between private benefits and social benefits for each user. Therefore, appropriate pricing is necessary to encourage users to remain with the system because of the positive externalities that are created. In both situations cited above, the fact remains, however, that traditional economic analysis must be modified to account for the externality problems that arise in network systems.

In the first essay, "Proliferation of Networks in Telecommunications," Professor Jerry A. Hausman argues that technological change has been the driving economic force leading to cost reductions for the two basic components of the network system: transmission capacity and switching. The emergence of fiber-optic cable, for example, has greatly reduced the cost of transmission in long-distance markets because fiber has virtually unlimited capacity. Once the cable is laid, the marginal cost of an additional message transmitted is close to zero. Similarly, there has been a decline in switching costs mainly because of advances in computer hardware and software technology. As Hausman notes, these changes have lead to greater use of transmission capacity and lowered use of switches in long-distance networks, and to greater use of switches and lowered use of transmission capacity in local networks. Similar technological developments explain the growth in cellular and local area networks, which Hausman calls overlay networks: network systems that are not fully integrated into a public telephone network system. As regulators and legislators debate policies designed to improve the efficiency of the system, it is perhaps instructive to consider the technological forces that are emerging, as well as the externality problem regarding changes in demand and supply that Boyer raises in his introduction.

In the second section of his essay, Hausman proposes the "imputation methodology" to guide regulators and legislators in setting prices for specific telecommunication services. This proposal, which has two parts, is based on the economic concepts of productive and allocative efficiency. The first part establishes a price floor for the "monopoly service elements" that a local exchange company (LEC) would sell to another telecommunications provider. The advantage that this approach offers is that the LEC would face the same cost as its competitors and, unless there were cost differences among the providers, would insure that the costs of providing these service elements are minimized. The second part requires regulators to set the access rate for long-distance services equal to long-run incremental cost, which would insure that resources are allocated efficiently. This policy is likely to solve the problem of using the existing network capacity efficiently, but leaves open the question of how to make investment decisions related to expanding capacity. Moreover, this may also increase the incentive for some high-volume customers to remain a part of the local telephone network.

The second essay in part 1, "The Efficiency of Market Coordination: Evidence from Wholesale Electric Power Pools," written by Professors Richard J. Gilbert, Edward Kahn, and Matthew White, examines the performance of power pools in wholesale markets to determine whether these markets are functioning efficiently. Recent changes in federal regulation have introduced elements of competition into the electric power industry. The Energy Policy Act, for example, has two key provisions in this regard. The first exempts power suppliers from the Public Utility Holding Act of 1935 and allows these suppliers to compete in different regulatory jurisdictions; the second mandates access to the transmission network, which permits buyers and sellers to contract separately for power generation and transmission services. Providing or maintaining access to the transmission network is important to increasing the availability of nonutility sources of power supply. However, mandating access may not necessarily lead to lower prices. Gilbert and Riordan

(1992) explain that unbundling (i.e., opening access to transmission) generation and transmission may actually lead to higher costs and, hence, higher prices for electricity because of the complementary relationship between these two components.[4] Thus, the likely success of these regulatory changes will partly depend on whether the transmission networks are operating efficiently.

Gilbert, Kahn, and White argue that power pools can improve economic efficiency in several ways. First, participants are better able to coordinate investment decisions, which to some extent internalizes the external costs that Boyer describes in his introduction. Second, members of the pool are able to share capacity to meet peak load demands and, therefore, each member can maintain a smaller level of reserve capacity. Again, this appears to be a solution to the externality problems that Boyer raises with respect to demand changes within a network system. The evidence Gilbert, Kahn, and White present for a sample of 277 utilities suggests, however, that there is no discernable difference between the performance of utilities that are members of a pool and that of those that are not. They conclude that mandating access to transmission networks may not improve efficiency since the wholesale power market appears to be functioning well.

In part 2, the focus shifts from the sources of network growth and efficiency to the effect of networks on competition within industries with a network present. In his introduction to this section, Professor Harry M. Trebing notes that networks are an important part of our social capital (or infrastructure), since networks increase productivity and, hence, raise our real incomes. He identifies the various efficiencies (e.g., from economies of scale and scope to better demand management) that are likely to be realized in network systems, but nevertheless suggests that networks may create high barriers to entry that allow providers to exercise market power in the provision of their services. Market power is the theme of Lee L. Selwyn's essay, "Market Failure in 'Open' Telecommunication Networks: Defining the New 'Natural Monopoly.' "

Selwyn's main argument is that firms seek to acquire market power and, once market power has been gained, firms attempt to erect entry barriers to maintain that market power. He asserts that networks in telecommunications yield significant cost advantages to common carriers over individual users, and to large common carriers over smaller specialized providers. In this context, he draws a connection between

---

4. See Richard Gilbert and Michael Riordan, "Regulating Complementary Products: A Problem of Institutional Choice," working paper, University of California, Berkeley, 1992.

the deregulation experience and development of hub-and-spoke networks in the airline industry and the likely evolution of competition in telecommunications in the event that similar public policies unfold in this sector. He argues, for example, that sunk costs associated with a telecommunication network make entry unlikely and that existing networks cannot be redeployed to new markets in response to profit opportunities. Consequently, these features make it possible for local service providers and interexchange providers to continue to dominate their markets. Selwyn concedes, however, that a series of connected networks is likely to evolve because of the emergence of new technologies, even though there are no obvious economies that stem from having these horizontally integrated. The conclusion that he reaches is that deregulation is not the solution and that continued regulation of service providers that control essential facilities is necessary to maintain and promote competition in the telecommunication sector.

The second essay in part 2, "Transformation in the Electric Utility Industry," is written by Professors Rodney Stevenson and Dennis Ray. They, like Selwyn, have some reservations regarding the benefits of complete deregulation. Stevenson and Ray review the emerging trends in regulatory policy at the federal and state levels, and foresee a potential conflict in the planned objectives of these regulatory changes. They surmise that federal regulators are relying primarily on market forces to determine a utility's growth and development while, at the same time, state regulators are adopting an integrated resource planning approach (one that involves a significant amount of control) to direct investment and resource allocation. Stevenson and Ray maintain that there is scope for both types of policies and that they need not conflict with one another, but suggest that additional safeguards be erected to ensure that the evolution of competition complements the integrated resource planning objectives.

In his introduction to the final part of this volume, Professor James L. Hamilton notes that the key issue is to find the optimal mix of competition and regulation for determining prices charged for network services. He argues that if the conditions are "right," competition is the appropriate public policy, but acknowledges that structural conditions can be misleading and may not be sufficient to make a determination. For example, if the threat of entry exists, providers will be unable to raise their prices significantly above the competitive level. However, where competition is not likely to emerge, he then suggests that regulation may be the best alternative.

In the first essay in part 3, Professors Jeffrey K. MacKie-Mason and Hal R. Varian discuss the various problems that arise when a specific telecommunication service is not priced appropriately. Their essay, "Some Economics of the Internet," examines the technological features of the Internet system, a network in which the economies of transmission and growing demand have greatly increased traffic. They raise a difficult question: How does one price a service where there is a mixture of private and public ownership of the network, and where the marginal cost of transmitting an additional message is virtually zero? They compare this situation to the classic economics problem of pricing a public good.

MacKie-Mason and Varian offer an interesting proposal for pricing the Internet, but the cost of their proposal may be prohibitive because of the nature of the technology involved. They propose that a continuous market for network availability of access to the backbone be established. In this setting, buyers register the maximum price that they are willing to pay for access and then attach that bid to the "packet" that they wish to transmit. Given that network capacity is fixed, a market-clearing bid is determined and all packets with bids exceeding this level will be transmitted. Indeed, the allocation described in the MacKie-Mason/Varian proposal corresponds to the equilibrium determined in a competitive marketplace.

The advantage that this mechanism offers is twofold. First, the "smart market" mechanism eliminates the congestion that generally occurs when there is a zero-price charge for usage or when there is excess demand at a positive price. One can imagine, as MacKie-Mason and Varian suggest, that the bid determines the route that the message takes. For example, packets with high bids are assigned fast routes while packets with low bids travel over slower routes. Moreover, parallel accounting systems could be used with the current system to allow for the use of an accounting system to determine price so as to not increase congestion at the routers. The second advantage is that the market clears as soon as bids are placed and, consequently, resources are used efficiently. The only real drawback appears to be that the technology necessary to implement the pricing mechanism has not been fully developed.

The second essay in this part, "Repeat-Buyer Programs in Network Industries," is written by Professor Severin Borenstein. He provides an explanation of specific pricing practices that permit incumbent firms in network industries to raise switching costs and, hence, deter entry. He cites programs used in the airline industry as one example, and argues that the concentration of flights at a specific hub allows an airline to offer a wider range of alternatives to its customers to earn frequent-flier miles as compared with some other airline, and that this locks those customers in to the airline operating the hub. Borenstein contrasts the airline example with some of the recent pricing strategies used in the telecommunication market. He acknowledges that, despite the presence of a network, the plans used by the long-distance carriers do not appear to be particularly well suited to giving a provider a competitive advantage. The difference seems to be that the telecommunication providers are unable to offer a wide range of different services to their customers that are not already available or that could not easily become available from competing providers.

One of the issues that emerges from the essays presented in this volume is that it is probably best for policy makers to seek a balance between deregulation and regulatory oversight. The authors of this volume are in agreement that market forces can be used to make resource allocation decisions, and that regulations should be designed to insure that competitive forces are likely to emerge and flourish in the network-related sectors. This, however, requires that regulators and legislators are willing to take major steps along the path of regulatory reform and to consider alternative means to achieve social goals that have heretofore served as the raison d'être for extant regulatory policy. Moreover, given the rapid pace of technological advance, policy makers must keep in mind the various ways that existing regulations have affected the evolution of networks and enact alternative regulations that are flexible and that can accommodate, not determine, the varied directions that technology will take in future years.

The experience in the telecommunication sector provides some insight into the potential problems that regulators and legislators are likely to confront in network-related industries as competition and technological change evolve over time. It is widely recognized that current pricing policies that were designed to cross-subsidize certain classes of customers have created an incentive for selected customers to seek alternative services from other providers. New technologies have made these alternatives cheaper and have lead to a rapid exodus from the existing network system. New competitors who enter these potentially lucrative market niches concentrate on attracting low-cost, high-volume customers. The consequence is that the local telecommunication provider is left serving the high-cost, low-volume customers under a regulatory structure that was designed to provide these customers service at a price below cost. Furthermore, the emergence of wireless technologies and the potential that cable television (CATV) providers will soon be in a position to offer audio and video telecommunication services indicate that different networks will soon be in competition with each other. This will partially alleviate the present problem that in order for competition to become a reality, especially in local exchange service markets, competitors must have access to the local network system. New technologies will allow new competitors to gain access to the existing customer base and compete without having access to the local network systems. Moreover, given the emergence of competition in the intra- and interLATA (local access and transport area) telecommunication service markets, it may be a propitious time for regulators and legislators to allow the Regional Bell Operating Companies (RBOCs) to compete against the new technologies under less onerous regulatory conditions. Ameritech's "Customers First" Plan, for example, is a carefully crafted proposal that would provide competitors with access to the local network and at the same time allow the RBOC to enter the market for interLATA services. This plan, combined with the pricing methodology outlined in Hausman's paper, would accomplish two goals: first, it would introduce more competition into the local exchange and interLATA service markets; and second, it would create a regulatory structure to insure that access to local exchange customers is available and, more importantly, that the service price is determined by the most efficient provider of that service.

The experience in the telecommunications sector indicates that there may be potential conflicts between various state and federal regulations that will have to be resolved as the market expands beyond a state's geographic boundaries. These conflicts are also beginning to surface in the electric power industry, as increased competition in generation and transmission makes it possible for buyers and sellers of electric power to transact across states with different regulatory standards. As Stevenson and Ray note in their essay, the different policy objectives at the state and federal levels will require tough political choices to be made to shape the future of the electric power industry.

The emerging public policy theme that stems from the essays in this volume is that as technological advances improve the efficiency of network systems and increase competition in various sectors of the economy, the entire regulatory structure, which was designed for a different era, will have to be changed dramatically. Fundamental changes must take place to allow the new technologies and increased competition to provide the full benefits to consumers. This may compel us to design new and innovative regulatory strategies that sustain the competitive process, and to abandon old regulatory strategies that attempt to determine the outcomes in the marketplace.

Part 1

Introduction to Part 1: Network Externalities

Kenneth D. Boyer

Transmission of electricity from one utility to another encounters the problem of parallel path flow. The essence of this problem is that it is impossible to transmit electricity directly from one point to another over a specified line if there are alternate routes that physically connect the generator and the user. For example, when the New York Power Pool contracts to buy electricity from Ontario Hydro, some of the electricity will travel directly across the Niagara Falls connection between the utilities. Some of the transmission will flow north of Lake Ontario into upper New York State. Some will travel across the Michigan/Ontario border, then around the western end of Lake Erie and back to New York over power lines owned by neither the buyer of the electricity nor the seller (see fig. 1). This flow of electricity can overload lines in Ohio and Pennsylvania, requiring additional capacity to be built there if the same service standard is to be maintained.

Pricing of the contract between Ontario and New York should take into account the external effects imposed on other utilities and their customers. This would be true for any externality, of course. One way of looking at network economies and diseconomies such as those in the situation just described is as a series of externalities. But is this a good way of dealing with network problems? Or does the fact that the externality is generated by network connections change the economic analysis of investment and regulation in a regular and predictable way? This topic lies at the heart of this book.

Production of services in networks is typical of all the classic regulated industries, not only power, telecommunication, and transportation. Many of the most interesting aspects of economic analysis in these industries come from the unexpected indirect influences that individual transactions have on others in a network. For example, consider the problem of port location. The decision by American President Lines (APL) to operate double-stack container trains out of the Port of Los

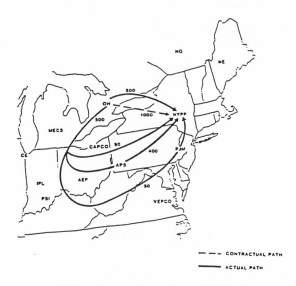

Fig. 1. Interconnected system response for Ontario Hydro to New York power pool 1,000 MW schedule. (From "ECAR/MAAC Interregional Power Transfer Analysis," ECAR/MAAC Coordinating Group, June 1985.)

Angeles had far-reaching consequences on other ports on the Pacific Coast; on other shipping companies; and on railroads connecting to ports other than the Port of Los Angeles; as well as on APL and the railroad who signed the contract. The success of the service has pulled additional sailings into the Port of Los Angeles, improving the quality of shipping service enjoyed by importers and exporters there. It has reduced sailings at ports in northern California, harming importers and exporters there; improved track maintenance along lines through southern Arizona, required for the traffic through Los Angeles; reduced the cost of carrying additional traffic on that line; and forced customers on other lesser-used lines, (for example, those through Utah) to bear a higher proportion of maintenance expenses than they otherwise would have.

In the state of Michigan, there was recently a bruising political battle over whether the single large railroad tunnel necessary to carry double-stack traffic between eastern Canada and the U.S. Midwest would be built in Port Huron or Detroit. The regulators' decision on where the tunnel would be built affected the fortunes not only of the Canadian National, CP Rail, Conrail, CSX, and Norfolk Southern but also shippers in different parts of Michigan. The effect on shippers came about due to the upgrading of some routes and downgrading of others that inevitably follows the decision on where the investment is placed.

These problems are in the same family as the power transmission problem described previously. Network problems differ from simple externality examples in the familiar parables of the beekeeper and the apple orchard or the upstream polluter and the downstream fisherman. In those stories, there are no indirect effects through other network paths; the third-party effects are clear, clean, easily traceable, easily assigned a cost figure (at least in principle), and potentially correctable. But in networks, buyers and sellers are connected with one another through multiple paths. Transactions between individual buyers and sellers are embedded in a web of transactions between other buyers (who are not identical to one another) and other sellers (who are similarly heterogeneous).

In a network, decisions made by buyers and sellers will have effects on others in the system, not only on the demand side but also on the supply side through changes in the quality of service or the cost of providing service to others. Changes in capacity of a network are always made to particular links and thus will affect buyers and sellers in a network unequally; in fact, changes in the capacity of one link, designed to improve service quality to some users of that network node, may well have the effect of worsening service quality to other users.

When an airline builds a hub, it is able to serve that city with aircraft that have lower costs per seat-mile, and it is also able to achieve a higher average load factor. By operating its system as a network, the airline becomes the low-cost supplier at the hub. These network economies can drain traffic from other hubs, however, increasing their costs and decreasing service frequency between outlying cities and the competing hub. So the decision to invest in one hub benefits some passengers and harms others, benefits one carrier and harms another. These effects are seen on the demand side and, through service frequency and aircraft usage, on the supply side as well.

Costs and service quality of serving a city pair depend on traffic carried on the airline between other city pairs and how the airline chooses to configure its traffic flow. It makes no sense, then, to analyze each city pair as a single market and try to calculate the costs of serving that market or the demand in that market, since, empirically, supply and demand influences from other markets will overwhelm the single-market data. Neither the concepts of common and joint costs nor the concept of economies of scope adequately covers the heterogeneity of service situations. Nor do they adequately deal with the interrelationships among consumers and among producers on both the supply and the demand side. The concepts are a clumsy way of dealing with the fact that capital increments do not affect all consumers equally. A successful network model has the promise of capturing all of these heterogeneities and interdependencies.

It is through infrastructure expansion that network effects are most likely to be seen. If the structure of a network remains constant, many of the network problems can be ignored. If there is insufficient capacity on a link at a particular time of day, for example, one can simply raise prices at that time to ration scarce capacity. This is the familiar solution to the problem of scarce runway capacity during peak periods at airports. But when the decision is made to expand capacity in a network, a necessary part of that decision is *where* the capacity increment should go; in other words, which links should benefit most directly and which links should not? Since classic economic models of congestion do not reflect the heterogeneity of users and of the infrastructure that they use, these models do not provide an answer to that question. If a bridge is operated independently of a road network, the capacity of the bridge should be increased when expected congestion tolls cover construction costs; but if there are several places where a new bridge could be sited, and if each site would benefit different groups of users differentially, merely calculating whether expected congestion tolls on current users exceed expansion costs at that site does not tell us where the bridge should go or when it should be built.

As noted previously, the traditional regulated sector consists of industries that have important network economies and diseconomies. Many of the most important decisions made by regulators—for example, who will pay for the improvement of the telephone network from voice grade to digital grade—are network-type decisions. In this case, the network aspects derive from the fact that the improvement in the infrastructure will benefit business users considerably more than residential users. Indeed, all problems of bypass in the telecommunication industry can be seen as a reflection of network problems. If there were no network aspects, then all customers would be identical and a capacity increment made by one customer would benefit all other customers equally. A more immediate network problem of regulation and capacity expansion is the case of how transmission capacity constraints in Idaho overload lines in Arizona that are used to carry power to customers in California. What is needed is a regulatory mechanism under which utilities in Idaho can be encouraged to build capacity of the appropriate type to alleviate lines in Arizona that are overloaded due to serving Californian demand. With regulators concerned only with small territories within a network structure, that mechanism does not now exist.

The essays that follow discuss problems of regulation and infrastructure building within networks. We need to learn how the heterogeneous interconnections among heterogeneous consumers and producers should be dealt with for the purpose of analyzing infrastructure and regulatory decisions in networks.

Proliferation of Networks in Telecommunications: Technological and Economic Considerations

Jerry A. Hausman

Networks are a common feature in telecommunications. However, networks are not an absolute requirement, since point-to-point connections are sometimes used. Thus, I first consider the question of why networks are so commonly used in telecommunications. The most straightforward economic answer is that point-to-point connection is usually too expensive to support telecommunications. Economic efficiency that causes the low-cost solution to be adopted typically favors networks over point-to-point solutions. A graphic example of the advantage of networks is given by the old-time pictures of lower New York City at the turn of the century, when numerous wires hung over the narrow streets, connecting buildings with each other and with the different telephone companies. Networks have the advantage that when a new customer joins the network, only one connection needs to be made instead of connections with the N already existing customers. Thus, networks grow at rate N, while point-to-point connections grow at rate N^2, which imposes a much higher cost on the system.

Telecommunication networks contain two essential elements: transmission capacity and switches. Transmission can be over copper wire, coaxial cable, fiber-optic cable (glass), or via radio transmission. The relative economic advantage among these transmission media depends on the use and is constantly changing due to changes in technology. Copper, historically the basis of the telephone network and still used extensively in the local component of the network, is very labor-intensive to install and offers relatively limited capacity. However, due to very recent developments in compression technology, the capacity of copper to carry data is growing extremely fast.[1] Thus, even the

1. Asymmetric digital subscriber line (ADSL), a technology being developed by Bellcore, currently allows the transmission of VCR-quality video to a customer premise

hundred-year-old transmission technology is greatly affected by changes in semiconductor electronics.

Fiber-optic cable, the transmission media that uses lasers to transmit ones and zeros of computer code over glass fiber, is the high-capacity transmission capacity of the present and future. Fiber uses computer electronics to create its capacity, and capacity has grown so rapidly with advances in computer technology that to a first approximation, it may not be too much of an exaggeration to say that the capacity of fiber is unlimited. Furthermore, the price of computer electronics to operate fiber transmission has been decreasing at the rate of about 10 percent per year for the last decade.

Radio transmission has a much lower labor component than either copper or fiber but typically offers poorer quality transmission and is often capacity constrained because of spectrum scarcity. However, digital radio technology, which is replacing the older analog technology, will improve the transmission quality greatly. Furthermore, the digital technology will also increase capacity. For instance, for cellular telephones the use of TDMA (time division multiplexing), now being installed, will increase the older analog capacity by a factor of 3 to 4. Code division multiplexing (CDMA), which is also close to adoption for cellular telephones, will increase capacity by 10 to 100 times over the analog technology. The U.S. government is also likely to increase the amount of spectrum available for telecommunication uses. Thus, the comparison among copper, fiber, and radio for a given use is in continuous flux as the effect of computer (digital) technology becomes incorporated into transmission systems.[2]

Switches, the other component of most telecommunication networks, decrease the need for transmission and provide interconnections with other networks. The original role of a switch was to decrease the amount of transmission required. A new customer requires only a single connection to a switch, rather than order N connections to the existing customers in the absence of a switch. Thus, a switch saves on the order of $N^2 - N$ connections, which creates a huge cost savings. A modern telecommunication switch is essentially a computer with a memory and a switch block. For a history of the development of modern digital tele-

---

that is sufficiently close to a central office. Within the past year the capacity of ADSL has approximately doubled while the distance from a central office to a customer premise has grown by about 50 percent. Bell Atlantic is currently conducting ADSL trials over its copper plant. Use of ADSL over copper will still require a significant incremental investment for its use.

2. See Calhoun 1992 for an optimistic assessment of the use of radio rather than copper or fiber transmission for nonmobile telecommunications application.

communication switches see Hausman and Kohlberg 1989. The economics of digital switches is basically driven by the economics of microprocessors and dynamic random access memory (DRAMs). Indeed, many central office switches use the same Intel X86 or Motorola processors as their main building blocks that are used in desktop and portable personal computers (PCs). The fundamental economic fact of central office switches is that prices are decreasing rapidly. In the last 10 years the price of a digital central office switch has decreased from about $240 per line to about $130 per line. Over the same period the price of a private branch exchange (PBX) has decreased from about $1,000 per port to about $300 per port. Again, the effect of computer technology on switch economics has been great.

Both transmission media and switches have decreased significantly in cost over the past decade. Their changing relative costs have led to different effects for different types of networks. In long-distance networks the decrease in fiber-optic cost per message has decreased the use of switching. For instance, predivestiture AT&T (pre-1984) had five levels of switches in its hierarchy.[3] The lowest-level switches, the Class 5 switches, remained with the BOCs (Bell Operating Companies) at divestiture. However, levels 1–4 from predivestiture AT&T Long Lines have been collapsed down to a single level in the hierarchy. Indeed, the change has been so profound that at least one recent study by Huber, Kellogg, and Thorne 1992 has concluded that long-distance service is a natural monopoly due to the overwhelming economies of scale created by fiber-optic transmission.

In local telephone networks, the decreasing cost of the switch has been the more important economic factor. Switches have decreased in size as well as in cost and can be seen as analogous to a PC. The formerly massive switches (e.g., mainframes) of the old Bell network have given way to minicomputer-sized switches. However, cellular companies and even the local exchange companies (LECs) have begun using more PC-sized switches called remotes. A remote switch can be put into the basement of a building, where the remote communicates to a larger switch via a fiber-optic connection. The use of remote switches leads to efficient collection of traffic and many fewer cables connecting the building and the central office. Remote switches are also increasingly being used by cellular providers and will be a crucial element in future Personal Communications Systems (PCS) networks. Within individual companies the decreasing cost of the PBX switch has been the primary factor

---

3. The switching hierarchy is described in Rey 1983, 107–10. In 1983 there were 9,800 Class 5 switches in the Bell system and 10 Class 1 switches.

in the proliferation of voice telecommunication networks. At the same time, data networks have also proliferated within companies using Local Area Networks (LANs). These LANs are connected to the outside world and to other networks through the use of telecommunication switches specially designed for data usage (e.g., routers).

Proliferation of New Networks

Prior to 1970 there was only the Bell network. AT&T provided about 80 percent of local telephone service and almost all long-distance service, both in the United States and internationally. Intracompany networks typically used Centrex, which operated through the central office switch and had a single transmission line between each port and the central office. PBXs were beginning to appear more frequently in 1970, but their processing capability and features were below those of Centrex and they were expensive. Regulation also had an important role in the single network outcome, but technology and economics were the main determinants.

PBX-Based Networks

In the 1970s PBXs led to the creation of the first significant number of non-Bell networks. Functionality and prices of PBXs both advanced greatly, especially beginning in 1975 with the introduction of digital PBXs by Rolm and Northern Telecom. Note that instead of each port being connected with the central office switch, the PBX collected the traffic and used only one line per 6 to 8 ports to connect to the central office switch. Thus, the PBXs represented a wide-scale substitution of switching for transmission capacity. Intracompany calls were switched by the PBX and were independent of the public switched telephone network (PSTN). PBXs not only created superior economics but also allowed for superior control by corporations. The element of control is an overlooked, but often important, factor. Indeed, the question exists whether large networks, offering diverse services, are inherently difficult to control. Large mainframe-based computer networks have exhibited similar difficulties. Very recently, public networks, with their greatly increased capacity due to the introduction of fiber optics together with more advanced intelligence introduced through computers, have begun to offer greater flexibility and better control by the individual customer. Once again, changes in technology have led to changes in the relative economics and likely changes in cost-efficient approaches to telecommunication services.

Intracompany Voice and Data Networks

Intracompany private networks became increasingly important beginning around 1980. These networks were first established to provide strategic advantage, rather than as a cost-minimizing economics approach. Citibank, Manufacturers Hanover, General Electric, and many other large corporations established networks to quicken their response and to increase access to information flows. McKenney and Nyce 1989 describe the strategy followed by Manufacturers Hanover in designing its network. However, these networks have not been able to provide a sustainable competitive advantage. Competitors were able to duplicate the network functionalities, often using the public network at lower cost. Indeed, with the advent of virtual private networks that use public network facilities, companies such as General Electric are dismantling their private networks and relying on the public carriers' facilities. Intracompany networks, whether they are based on private facilities or public network facilities, still remain a competitive necessity, even if they cannot provide sustainable competitive advantage. Bradley, Hausman, and Nolan 1993 discuss the increasing importance of these intracompany networks as a response to globalization and the increasing importance of intracompany information flows. Indeed, a common estimate is that about 50 percent of U.S. corporate investment from 1986–92 went to information technology and telecommunication equipment. I expect these investments to increase further as company networks become increasingly important competitive strategy tools.

Interexchange Carrier (IXC) Networks

MCI and Sprint, followed by Wiltel, have constructed fiber-optic long-distance networks that compete with AT&T for long-distance traffic.[4] AT&T began to install digital switches and fiber-optic transmission in its Long Lines (long-distance) network in the late 1970s and early 1980s. However, the industry's conversion from coaxial copper cable to fiber accelerated in the late 1980s with the rapidly decreasing cost and increasing capacity of fiber and the successful "pin drop" marketing campaign of Sprint. All three major carriers have now installed essentially all-fiber-optic networks. Abundant capacity exists due to the constantly increasing capacity of fiber. Indeed, a 1989 FCC study found that non-AT&T carriers could supply about 150 percent of all long-distance minutes, although

---

4. An additional 12 or so regional networks also exist, although consolidation is occurring fairly rapidly among regional carriers.

AT&T had about two-thirds of industry output.[5] It is interesting, and perhaps ironic, that microwave technology, which provided the technological justification for MCI's entry into long distance, became technologically obsolete for long-distance networks within about 10 years of MCI's entry. Of course, technology provides only one component of competitive outcomes.

Cellular Networks and PCS Networks

Cellular networks provide the success story of the last decade in terms of increased telecommunication network usage. Cellular telephone service began in the United States in Chicago and Los Angeles in 1984. Cellular networks were the first networks designed for an increasingly mobile U.S. population. Cellular telephone networks divided geographical areas up into hexagonal cells so that the scarce radio frequencies, which are the transmission media, can be reused. As a car passes from one cell into another cell the cellular telephone call is switched from one frequency to another frequency. Cellular networks demonstrate the importance of high functionality and low-cost switching capability.

At first, each separate cellular operation (in a metropolitan statistical area [MSA] or rural statistical area [RSA]) had its own switch. However, consolidation of operations (e.g., McCaw in Florida) and the development of low-cost remote switches have led to fewer switches with better interconnection via fiber-optic cable. This proliferation of cellular networks would have occurred even more quickly except for regulation-induced barriers, in particular the application of the 1984 Modification of Final Judgment (MFJ) of the AT&T divestiture to the operations of BOC cellular operations.

Growth of the cellular telephone industry has been extremely rapid. Growth rates of 30–40 percent per year have occurred during the late 1980s and early 1990s. The federal government has made many individuals, such as John Kluge, and corporations, such as the Washington Post, along with the BOCs, extremely wealthy by giving away the cellular frequencies. Hopefully this mistake will not be repeated in the future when the FCC assigns PCS frequencies. Auctions (or giveaways with unlimited resale, which is equivalent to a secondary auction) are the only economically efficient procedure. No reason exists that the government should make some lucky individual extremely well off through a spectrum lottery. For instance, the Cape Cod cellular license was resold for $40 million by the lottery winner of the frequency. Government

---

5. See Haring 1989.

auctions will allow for use of the auction proceeds to reduce the need for increased taxes to solve other fiscal problems.

To date, cellular has been a complement, not a substitute, to the public network. While cellular is a stand-alone network for mobile-to-mobile calls, more than 90 percent of the total calls go over the PSTN. However, the situation could change in the future as penetration of cellular networks (and PCSs) increases. Cellular is now up to about a 5 percent penetration level. However, capacity limitations in large cities such as Los Angeles and New York, as well as high prices, have limited penetration. Capacity limitations will quickly recede in importance. TDMA, time division digital multiplexing, is currently being installed and increases capacity by 3 to 4 times. CDMA, code division digital multiplexing, will increase capacity by 10 to 100 times. Both will lead to superior quality transmission because they will replace analog radio transmission with digital transmission ("pin drop" quality).

The federal government will soon increase capacity with PCS. While PCS is still a vaguely defined group of services, at least one form of PCS is likely to be an advanced cellular type of service. At a minimum the FCC will probably license three new competitors which will increase the number of mobile providers from two to five (or three to six in cities where FleetCall is present). Increased capacity and more competitors should lead to lower prices and increased competition for mobile telecommunication services. However, the extent of the price decrease is unclear because of the uncertainty of the cost of PCS networks. Initial optimism has waned due to the realization of the significant costs of constructing PCS networks. However, changes in technology may well decrease the current costs quite rapidly in the future. PCS is likely to use other networks, such as cable networks, as well as the PSTN to provide the network backbone. Thus, as cellular penetration increases, the proportion of telephone calls that do not use the PSTN will increase. This change will have important implications for the economics and regulation of the PSTN.

Competitive Access Providers (CAPs)

Competitive Access Providers (CAPs) are another recent introduction of telecommunication networks. Residential telephone service was cross-subsidized in the predivestiture Bell system and continues to be cross-subsidized today, although to a lessened extent. By cross subsidy I mean that the price of monthly residential telephone service is priced below the incremental (marginal) cost of providing the service. After divestiture intra-AT&T transfers could no longer take place. A charge for transmission from customer premises to the central office switch and then to an interexchange carrier (IXC) such as AT&T or MCI was instituted, called an access charge. The access charge was used to replace the predivestiture subsidy flows. The FCC subsequently also adopted a fixed monthly charge, the subscriber line charge (SLC), which was used to fund residential telephone service. The current SLC for residential lines is $3.50 per month. The current access charge is about $0.035 cents per minute, with the cost of providing the service between $0.005 and $0.01 cents per minute (for originating and terminating access). The regulation-induced difference between the price of access and the cost of access allowed for competitive service offerings, which worked together with more sophisticated PBXs at customer locations. Competitors soon began to offer alternative access-provision services.

Teleport was the first CAP, beginning operation in Manhattan in 1984. Teleport used a fiber-optic network that provided greater reliability at lower cost to large businesses. Interestingly, Teleport was essentially a switchless network that provided only transmission from the customer premise to the IXC point of presence (POP). CAPs operate economically only in very dense population situations. Capacity of fiber optics could lead to a "switchless network" if capacity continues to increase sufficiently, for example, like current cable networks, where each caller pulls off its own message from the torrent of digital information carried over the fiber-optic cable.

CAPs have spread to 24 of the 25 largest cities, with great plans for future expansion. Teleport (originally Merrill Lynch and now owned by Cox Cable and TCI) and MFS (recently offered to the public in an initial public offer [IPO]) are the two primary competitors. Somewhat surprisingly, Teleport and MFS have gone head to head in most major cities. Although it is difficult to tell definitively, the CAPs have not been profitable to date. Merrill Lynch had Teleport on the block for two years before selling the company. Also, early aggressive expansion plans have been curtailed. CAPs are very capital-intensive operations, and the local exchange companies (LECs) have responded with their own competitive fiber rings in large cities.

Future prospects for CAPs are unclear. CAPs were recently the beneficiary of an interconnection ruling from the FCC that allows them to use LEC facilities to transport (nonswitched) traffic to and from less dense areas where CAP's networks do not reach. Furthermore, CAP networks could be used as backbone networks for PCSs in central business districts. Presumably, this consideration explains the interest and significant investment in Teleport by Cox and TCI, who could combine their cable properties with CAP networks to provide metropolitan PCS services. Also, if upgraded cable TV networks begin to offer voice-grade telephone services, as has already begun in the United Kingdom, as well as interactive information services, CAPs would be the service provider in central business districts.

MFS has also announced that it will offer high-capacity long-distance service connecting the 15 cities in which it currently operates. However, the MFS strategy is quite a risky one, since AT&T and the other IXCs provide about two-thirds of CAP demand through LEC bypass for large business customers. Another potential problem for the CAPs is that under the new FCC transport rules, the IXCs will be able to provide their own unswitched transport using LEC central office facilities. "Do-it-yourself" bypass, especially from AT&T, could be a major threat to the future success of the CAPs.

Local Area Networks (LANs)

Local Area Networks (LANs) that connect computers, mainly PCs, are another recent development. Before the 1970s there were only a few mainframes (large switches), so that data was transmitted to a mainframe either through a dumb terminal (e.g., an IBM 3270) or by walking a deck of cards over to the computer center (e.g., self-transmission). As computing power became much less expensive and minicomputers and PCs began to take over, computing power became much more widely distributed. The PC now plays the role of a telecommunication switch with the ultimate in decentralization where every user has control of a switch. However, for users who still want connection, a ring network design, rather than the traditional star network design, is used. The ring network topology is the limiting outcome for a network design when switching costs approach zero for a finite transmission cost. My description here is an oversimplification because switch costs are not really zero. Nevertheless, costs of managing mainframes became too high because they seemingly could not be managed efficiently. It became more efficient to provide each user with a private switch, rather than trying to share a large communal switch.

LANs, when they connect with outside networks, often to provide wide area networks (WANs), do so through PBX switches that are specially designed for high-speed data applications (routers). Traffic concentration is again important because one does not require an outside transmission line for each computer. Even more important for data traffic, because of the use of packet switching for data applications, it leads to much more efficient transmission usage. The ratio of 6 to 8 ports to one outside transmission line for voice traffic can easily become 100 to 200 to one for a packet-switched network.

Overlay Networks and Interconnection

All of the new networks I have discussed do their own intranetwork transmission without relying on the PSTN. This intranetwork transmission feature leads me to call them *overlay,* rather than integrated, networks. These networks, at least to some degree, forgo economies of scope. But, in turn, the networks achieve increased autonomy and gain improved manageability. The United States is achieving network redundancy, although at a cost. This proliferation of networks might not have happened without the divestiture of AT&T, but the speed of change (dynamic efficiency) is much greater because the extremely long delays, inherent in the regulatory process, have either been eliminated or at least significantly attenuated.

An important outcome of the proliferation of networks is a tremendous increase of access nodes into the PSTN. No longer do you need your telephone handset to be connected into the local loop to gain access to the PSTN. Instead, you can enter the PSTN from another switch where you have already been aggregated with a lot of other traffic to achieve economies of scale in transmission. These other networks will be both complements and substitutes (competitors) of the PSTN. We badly need regulatory rules to establish access terms to the PSTN. We also need to establish rules for access charges to set the price for access. So long as the PSTN is a common carrier, competitors will demand access on "fair" terms and conditions. However, an interesting question does arise from these many new networks. If the current bottleneck is eliminated because of radio (PCS) access and cable access, should the PSTN still be regulated as a common carrier? Or, conversely, should the PCS and cable networks be regulated as common carriers? However, for now the PSTN still has market power and will continue to be regulated. Thus, I move on from these potentially important questions to develop the proper regulatory rules to set prices for access to the PSTN.

Access Rules, and Prices for Connection to the PSTN

All of these overlay networks will require access to the PSTN to connect to other networks. The terms and conditions, that is, access rules and prices, are often matters of significant dispute among parties. Regulators typically become involved in determining appropriate terms and conditions. However, the correct basis for determining appropriate terms and conditions is not always clear. Here I set forth an approach that should allow for network access and determine appropriate prices for access that will allow for the overlay networks such as cellular and

PCS operators, the IXCs for intraLATA services, and the CAPs to compete with the LECs. I develop a method for setting the terms and conditions called the "imputation methodology." Two principles are involved in the imputation methodology; both principles are based on the goal of economic efficiency. Economic efficiency should be the primary goal of regulation, so that the economy can operate in the most efficient manner.[6]

The imputation methodology corresponds to the economic principle of productive economic efficiency so that the low-cost producer, either the LEC or the new competitor, can set its price to reflect cost. Competitors are not disadvantaged when they purchase "monopoly building block" services and economic efficiency is assured.[7] Note that the imputation methodology should only be used for monopoly service elements. If a service is supplied competitively, no need for the imputation methodology is present.

The imputation rule states that an LEC will be required to provide "monopoly service elements" where the price it charges to competitors is imputed into its own price for competing services, with cost differences in providing the monopoly service element being recognized so that economic efficiency is achieved. Recognition of cost differences in imputing access charges into the price of the LEC service is an important component of ensuring economic efficiency. Thus, if the LEC can serve itself at a lower cost than a competitor (for example, an IXC that goes through a tandem switch for long-distance access to its POP while a LEC doesn't), the imputation rule needs to account for the cost difference. Competitors often argue that the LECs should impute the same price as the tariff rate they are charged, but this argument is incorrect if cost differences are present. If cost differences are not taken into account, economic efficiency will not be achieved.

Application of the Imputation Methodology

The imputation methodology sets the price floor for an LEC service. The LEC cannot price below this amount or economic inefficiency will be the result. Of course, the imputation methodology only sets a floor, and actual prices can be higher depending on competitive market conditions. The imputation methodology leads to the following imputation

---

6. The California Public Utilities Commission (CPUC) established economic efficiency as the first of its goals in 1987. Other goals, such as universal service, also need to be accounted for, in addition to economic efficiency.

7. By a monopoly building block I mean a service provided by an LEC that cannot be provided economically by a competitor to the LEC.

rule: price floors are determined by summing the incremental cost of the *LEC's service* and the contribution (price – incremental cost) contained in the price of monopoly building blocks the *competitors buy* to provide a competitive service.[8] The tariff rate for monopoly building block services, such as access, will often be set above incremental cost so that a contribution is made to the joint and common costs of the network, but the imputation methodology ensures that the LEC does not receive a competitive advantage from this pricing policy. The LEC price for the competitive service will reflect the price of the monopoly building block service provided to the competitor, but it will do so to ensure economic efficiency.

Imputation is no longer required when a competitive service exists as an alternative to the monopoly building block service. In fact, it is then not a monopoly building block service. The price of the service will be "reasonable" or it will not be a competitive offering. Thus, an imputation rule is not required in this situation. For example, in situations where competitors do not necessarily purchase an (originating) switched access service from an LEC (e.g., AT&T Megacom, where CAP access is often used), the LEC will not be required to impute the switched access tariff rate at the HiCap end; instead, the price floor will be comprised of the overall incremental cost for the LEC's competing service plus the contribution from switched access at the terminating end. Any monopoly elements of such a service, such as terminating switched access or originating special access (to the extent that it is considered not to be competitive), will still be subject to the imputation formula. For example, for customers whose usage makes Megacom an economic alternative, an LEC might well be permitted to offer a competing switched access message toll service (MTS) with a price floor at the incremental cost of the entire service plus contributions from terminating switched access where an imputation would occur.

The Imputation Rule: Some Examples

I now present three examples that demonstrate how the imputation methodology works. First, consider the case in which the LEC's toll service will compete with IXC services for low-volume customers. Suppose the rates and costs for toll and access charges are as displayed in table 1.

To calculate the LEC's toll price floor under the imputation methodology, I employ the following procedure: First, add the switched access

---

8. By incremental cost I refer to the use of long-run incremental cost (LRIC).

TABLE 1. Imputation Methodology for the Case of Switched Access

	Incremental Cost per Minute	Rate (Price) per Minute
Originating switched access	$0.005	$0.0166
Terminating switched access	$0.005	$0.0480
LEC's toll (access elements)	$0.008	
LEC's toll (nonaccess elements)	$0.012	

rate (both originating and terminating) to the LEC's *cost* for nonaccess elements. This calculation produces a floor of $0.0766 ($0.0166 originating switched access rate + $0.0480 terminating switched access rate + $0.012 nonaccess cost element). Note that if no cost differences exist, this procedure places the LEC in the same position as its competitor, so that the more efficient company with respect to the nonaccess elements will be in a position to set a lower price. Second, the LEC can adjust the floor for any difference in costs between providing access to itself and providing switched access to competing carriers. In my example, this cost advantage equals $0.002 ($0.005 originating switched access cost + $0.005 terminating switched access cost − the LEC's $0.008 cost for toll access elements). Thus the price floor for the LEC becomes $0.0746 ($0.0766 − $0.002).

Note that the outcome of the two-part calculation is exactly the same as that obtained by using the economic principle of adding together the LEC's incremental cost of toll and the contribution paid by its competitors.[9] The two approaches are mathematically identical so that the particular method used to calculate the imputed price floors is solely a choice based on convenience, not on different economic principles. More importantly, both the LEC and the competitor that depends on the use of the monopoly building block service element are placed in a similar economic position, so that the firm with the lower cost of providing the nonaccess elements of the service will have a lower cost basis for the entire service. So long as regulators establish the correct rules, the company with the lower cost basis will be in a position to charge the lower price. Thus, economic efficiency will be the result, since the firm with the lower cost basis will be able to charge the lower price for the service in question.

For my next example, I consider services for large-volume customers,

---

9. In my example, the contribution per minute in the switched access rates is $0.0546 ($0.0166 originating rate + $0.0480 terminating rate − $0.005 originating cost − $0.005 terminating cost). When added to the LEC's *total* incremental cost for a toll of $0.02 ($0.008 access + $0.012 nonaccess), the floor becomes $0.0746, exactly the same as before.

for which IXCs use dedicated nonswitched access (i.e., special access) at the originating end of the call. In applying the equal contribution principle, the contribution per minute for this *special* access is the correct component at the originating end, if competitive alternatives to special access do not exist, even though the LEC's competitive service is MTS high-volume discount plans. For example, if the LEC's high-capacity access rate is $625 per T-1 facility (DS-1) and a typical customer generates 50,000 minutes per month, the average rate per minute is $0.0125 ($625/50,000). If the incremental cost of special access is, say, $350 per month, then the average contribution per minute is $0.0055. Thus, the contribution paid by IXC competitors averages $0.0485 per minute ($0.0055 originating + $0.0430 terminating). The LEC's price floor for high-volume services would then be $0.0685 ($0.02 cost + $0.0485 contribution).

The above example assumes high-capacity access is not competitive and is therefore considered a monopoly building block. My last example occurs when high-capacity access services are competitive. The LEC would not be required to include a contribution associated with originating access. In a competitive situation, competing intraLATA carriers would no longer be dependent on the LEC for originating access—that is, originating access would not be a monopoly element. Instead, the competing intraLATA carrier could purchase the service from a CAP. Thus the equal contribution principle results in a floor of $0.0630 ($0.02 cost + $0.0430 contribution for terminating switched access).

Regulatory Price Setting for Access

My development of the imputation rule depends on the tariff price. Where does this tariff price come from? The tariff price is usually set by the regulator, either the FCC for interstate access or by a state regulator for intrastate access, because if it is a "monopoly building block service" the LEC has market power and the rate will be regulated. I next turn to the correct economic principles that should guide regulatory price setting for access tariffs.

Principles of correct regulation should account for economic efficiency when setting access prices. As I discussed above, the access price, at both the federal and state levels, is set well above its cost to fund the cross subsidy for residential service. The contribution from the access charges is also used to pay for joint and common costs of networks. To apply economic efficiency we now consider the second type of economic efficiency—allocative economic efficiency. To increase economic efficiency, regulators should lower access prices toward their incremental cost. The main gain in economic efficiency occurs because long-distance prices fall and long-distance demand has a relatively high price elasticity, between about 0.3 and 1.1, depending on the type of call, with the bounds being set by intraLATA and international calls. Thus the quantity of long-distance calls will increase significantly, leading to increased economic efficiency.[10]

Now a decrease in the cross subsidy for residential service is sometimes claimed to have adverse effects on another goal of regulators besides economic efficiency—universal service. However, targeted subsidies for low-income households such as "lifeline" services have been implemented over the past decade. No general cross subsidy to *all* households, as now occurs, serves any useful policy purpose. Furthermore, a change that would decrease or eliminate the residential cross subsidy need not lead to a decrease in the universal service goal. Hausman, Tardiff, and Belinfante (1993) have recently demonstrated that the increase in local telephone rates during the 1980s, which was accompanied by a decrease in long-distance prices mainly due to decreased access charges, did *not* lead to a decrease in telephone penetration. Instead, the combination of lifeline service packages and lower long-distance rates actually led to an increase in telephone penetration during the 1984–90 time period.

However, another way to consider the problem of regulatory price setting for access charges relates to the first type of economic efficiency that I discussed—productive efficiency. Diamond and Mirrlees 1971 prove that, under fairly general conditions that are likely to be satisfied in the U.S. economy, to achieve productive economic efficiency the government (or regulators) should not set prices of intermediate production goods to exceed costs (i.e., inputs to the productive process for final goods or services). The essential economic idea is that if prices exceed costs for an input of production, economic efficiency is decreased because a producer will then shift to a lower-priced, but potentially higher-cost, input because its price is lower.[11] But economic efficiency states that the lowest *cost* input should be used or society's resources are wasted. Thus, this loss of productive efficiency adds another component to the overall loss in economic efficiency caused by the current access rate structure.

To achieve the goal of setting access price equal to its incremental

---

10. About 35–45 percent of the IXC's revenues are used to pay for access charges.

11. Interestingly, much of the debate over the Clinton administration's proposed BTU tax (1993) arises from these same considerations, as suppliers of different fuels attempt to gain a favored position.

TABLE 2. Approximate Changes in the Average SLC to Balance Elimination of the Joint and Common Component of Access Charge

	Increase in SLC	
Current Access Component	With GSF[a]	Without GSF
IC (Interconnect)	$1.90 per month	$1.60 per month
CCL	$1.50 per month	$1.95 per month

[a] This increase includes moving the GSF Part 69 cost allocation proposed by the FCC in CC Docket 92-222 into the SLC.

cost we will need to raise the rate of some other LEC services so that the LEC can earn its cost of capital, that is, the LEC needs to earn a return on the joint and common (nonincremental) costs of the network. The obvious best choice is to increase the subscriber line charge (SLC), which is almost like a lump-sum tax, so it has almost no adverse efficiency consequences.[12] I therefore estimate by how much the SLC will need to increase, *at the federal level,* for interstate access rates to be set at incremental cost, given the current separations process.[13] In table 2, I calculate the approximate change in the SLC that will permit setting the interstate access price at incremental cost while increasing the SLC to make the outcome approximately revenue-neutral. Thus, the amount of the required increase in the SLC is just about $3.50 per month. We would need to approximately double the SLC from its current level, an increase of about $2.50 per month over the inflation-adjusted amount originally set by Congress. I calculate the efficiency gain, at the federal level alone, for residential customers to be over $1.1 billion per year from the lowering of long-distance prices due to lower access prices together with the increase in the SLC.[14] Thus, we are suffering a large

12. The price elasticity of local service is typically estimated to be less than 0.05.

13. The separations process divides the network into separate federal and state components for accounting and regulatory purposes. The separations process borders on the bizarre, with details that only an accountant could appreciate. Most telecommunication policy makers agree that the separations process needs to be significantly modified because of changes in technology and regulation. Approximately 25 percent of an LEC's capital is usually assigned to federal regulation, although a much higher proportion of access charges are set by the FCC. The actual proportion varies by state.

14. This calculation is based on interstate long distance minutes as reported by the FCC in its 1992 report and a price elasticity for interstate calls of 0.723 that has been used by the FCC in recent determinations. Note that an additional efficiency loss is currently being created by state regulators setting access prices for intrastate interLATA long distance well above incremental cost. Indeed, many state regulators use the FCC tariffs in setting these access prices. A further efficiency loss arises from the high imputed or explicit access prices used for intrastate intraLATA calls.

efficiency loss unnecessarily. This large loss in economic efficiency could be remedied without a loss in universal service, so long as targeted subsidies, such as lifeline service, are used in the appropriate manner. Furthermore, both the LECs, who would be better able to compete with emerging access competition, and IXCs, whose lower access costs would lead to increased long-distance demand, would benefit from this change, along with consumers, who would receive the benefit of significantly lower long-distance prices.

Conclusions

Technology will cause the continued proliferation of telecommunication networks. Within the next decade I expect to see multiple PCS networks, at least one, and perhaps more, broadband networks, and increased numbers of CAP networks, LANs, and WANs. New types of telecommunication networks, only dimly foreseen today, will also come into being. Consumer benefits will arise if these various networks are interconnected. New services will be provided and increased network redundancy may create marginal additional benefits.

However, regulatory rules that set the terms for access and set price floors for regulated companies to ensure economic efficiency must be established. Cellular telephone was delayed in the United States for 10 to 15 years because of regulatory wrangling; a repeat performance for PCS and other new technologies would be a national tragedy. The correct regulatory approach will increase economic efficiency in two respects. First, productive economic efficiency can be created by causing the least-cost access technology and network configuration to be used. Also, large gains in allocative efficiency will occur if price is moved down toward the cost for access. The gains in allocative economic efficiency are well in excess of $1 billion per year. Thus, regulation must be updated to allow for the reality of complementary and competing networks that will perhaps become the most important economic factor for telecommunication policy in the coming years.

REFERENCES

Bradley, S. P., and J. A. Hausman, eds. 1989. *Future Competition in Telecommunications*. Boston: Harvard Business School Press.
Bradley, S. P., J. A. Hausman, and R. L. Nolan, eds. 1993. *Globalization, Technology, and Competition*. Boston: Harvard Business School Press.
Calhoun, G. 1992. *Wireless Access and the Local Telephone Network*. Boston: Artech House.

Diamond, P. A., and J. A. Mirrlees. 1971. "Optimal Taxation and Public Production, I: Production Efficiency." *American Economic Review* 61, no. 1: 8–27.

Haring, J. 1989. "What Makes the Dominant Firm Dominant?" OPP working paper no. 25.

Hausman, J. A., and E. Kohlberg. 1989. "The Future Evolution of the Central Office Switch Industry." In *Future Competition in Telecommunications,* ed. S. P. Bradley and J. A. Hausman. Boston: Harvard Business School Press.

Hausman, J. A., T. Tardiff, and A. Belinfante. 1993. "The Effects of the Breakup of AT&T on Telephone Penetration in the U.S." *American Economic Review* 83, no. 2: 178–90.

Huber, P. W., M. K. Kellogg, and J. Thorne. 1992. *The Geodesic Network II: 1992 Report on Competition in the Telephone Industry.* Washington, D. C.: The Geodesic Co.

McKenney, J. L., and H. E. Nyce. 1989. "The Role of the Large Corporation in the Communications Market." In *Future Competition in Telecommunications,* ed. S. P. Bradley and J. A. Hausman. Boston: Harvard Business School Press.

Rey, R. F. 1983. *Engineering and Operations in the Bell System.* 2d ed. Murray Hill, N.J.: AT&T Bell Laboratories.

The Efficiency of Market Coordination: Evidence from Wholesale Electric Power Pools

Richard J. Gilbert, Edward Kahn, and Matthew White

Background

The Public Utility Regulatory Policies Act of 1978 (PURPA) opened the door to competition in electric power by defining a new class of nonutility electricity generators, called qualifying facilities, with rights to sell to investor-owned utilities at regulated rates. Although considered by many a watershed act in the deregulation of electric power in the United States, PURPA's effect on the industry was only incremental, for two reasons. First, PURPA restricted qualifying facility status to small producers using renewable fuels and to cogenerators. Second, PURPA did not promote change in the vertically integrated structure of the industry. Qualifying facilities could sell only to the utility in the service area in which they were located.

The Energy Policy Act enacted in October of 1992 is the most significant legislation affecting the electricity market since the Public Utility Regulatory Policies Act and has the potential for more fundamental change. The Energy Policy Act fills more than 350 pages in the *Federal Register* and covers subjects that range from efficiency standards for hot water storage tanks to alternative-fueled vehicles. The sections of the Energy Policy Act with the greatest implications for competition in this industry are those that amend the Public Utility Holding Company Act of 1935 and parts of the PURPA that deal with the Federal Energy Regulatory Commission's (FERC) authority to mandate transmission access.

Although long entrenched in policy involving transmission access, the FERC had construed its authority in this area to be limited.

The authors are grateful for financial support from the University of California Energy Institute.

Accordingly, disputes over access have been settled in the Courts, as in the case of Otter Tail Power Co. (1973), where the Supreme Court held that denying transmission access to a local municipality was an unlawful exercise of a utility's market power. Otter Tail and related cases, however, have not resulted in wide-reaching rules governing the provision of access.

Under the PURPA reform of 1978, the FERC had the authority to mandate transmission access, but only if such access

1. is in the public interest;
2. conserves energy, improves reliability, or increases efficiency;
3. does not result in any undue burden, impair ability to render adequate service, or create uncompensated economic loss;
4. does not interfere with existing competitive relationships; and
5. does not result in retail wheeling.

According to Jurewitz 1993, the fourth condition was regarded as a "deal killer" and the FERC has never ordered wheeling under these provisions. More recently, the FERC has used transmission access as a carrot for approval of utility mergers, as in the merger of Utah Power and Light and Pacific Power and Light, and that of Northeast Utilities with the ill-fated Public Service of New Hampshire. In these cases, the FERC did not mandate access, but rather made it clear that transmission access would be a condition for FERC approval of the merger.

The success of power production from qualifying facilities has led many state regulatory commissions to expand the universe of potential suppliers to include additional nonutility sources of supply. However, much concern was expressed that the long-term effectiveness of an independent power sector would depend on guaranteed access to transmission services. The Energy Policy Act advanced the development of independent power by making certain nonutility generators exempt from the provisions of the Public Utility Holding Act of 1935, which restricted the ability of electricity suppliers to operate in different regulatory jurisdictions. These "exempt wholesale generators" are entities that are engaged exclusively in the production of electricity for sale in wholesale markets. In addition, the Energy Policy Act (EPA) gave the FERC expanded powers to mandate transmission access. Under the EPA, the FERC could mandate transmission access if

1. voluntary negotiations have been conducted by the requesting entity and transmission owner for 60 days,
2. the order will be in the public interest,

3. reliability of all utility systems affected by the order will be maintained, and
4. third-party wheeling is not subsidized by utility's existing customers.

In particular, this amendment deletes the onerous requirement that transmission access not "interfere with existing competitive relationships."

Whether the Energy Policy Act will enhance the performance of the U.S. electricity market depends on the present performance of the wholesale market and on how the FERC and state regulators implement the access provisions of the act. This essay looks broadly at both of these issues. The mandating of transmission access will allow wholesale buyers and sellers to contract separately for bulk power and transmission services. First, we present an overview of the regulatory costs and benefits of unbundling these two components of electricity supply. Then we examine the efficiency of the existing wholesale market. Institutions currently exist that provide varying degrees of wholesale market access to their members. These "power pools" range from loose structures of affiliated utilities to highly coordinated organizations that mimic the operations of a centralized firm and effectively guarantee access to their members. The data described in this section show only limited evidence that these more formal pools achieve greater efficiencies in their use of generation assets, although they may have some positive impact on investment. The implication is that, at least for transactions involving assets already in place, the present U.S. wholesale market appears to be reasonably efficient in the use of these assets. The consequences of this result for the implementation of the Energy Policy Act are discussed briefly in the concluding section.

Is Unbundling a Good Idea?

The movement toward open access to electricity transmission markets parallels the trend in other regulated industries toward unbundling the regulated product and limiting regulation to certain core activities. Examples are the unbundling of local and long-distance telephone services and the unbundling of natural gas production from natural gas transportation.

An argument that is advanced for unbundling is that it promotes competition in markets that do not have natural monopoly characteristics and therefore improves market performance. This argument ignores the possibility that unbundling may aggravate the information asymmetries that are faced by the regulator, and in this manner lead to outcomes that are worse than with a producer of a bundled product.

Gilbert and Riordan 1992 address the question of the regulatory benefits of unbundling when regulated services are produced using complementary inputs. Suppose that it takes one unit of an input with cost α (this can be bulk power generation) and one unit of another input with cost β (this can be transmission services) to produce one unit of a final product. The unit cost of the final product is $C(\alpha,\beta) = \alpha + \beta = \gamma$. If a regulated firm produces the bundled product, the regulator's information problem concerns the magnitude of the total cost, γ. The regulator's optimal policy for this situation is a standard application of the theory advanced by Baron and Myerson 1982, Laffont and Tirole 1993, and others.

Suppose instead that the regulator divides production into two, unbundled components, each supplied by one regulated firm. Now the regulator has to deal with the private information held by each of two different suppliers of the two components. Each supplier, acting independently, will negotiate with the regulator considering his actual cost (e.g., the cost of bulk power) and the expected cost of the input produced by the other supplier (e.g., transmission services). Gilbert and Riordan 1992 show that this behavior leads to an expected cost for the final product (delivered power) that is higher than would occur when a single producer owns both factors of production. Unbundling results in a negative competitive externality when inputs are complements. This would make the regulator worse off if unbundling did nothing to lower the cost of production of one (or both) of the inputs. If an industry is structurally competitive, unbundling should result in lower costs, although the cost reduction will depend on the extent to which the integrated firm exploits the competitive technology. The implication of this research is that regulators should not expect unbundling to improve their lot unless they can expect a substantial increase in competition in one or both of the unbundled products.

Should Transmission Be Regulated at All?—Results on Power Pools

In the search for new ways to enhance competition in wholesale electricity markets, a natural question to begin with is whether competition in wholesale markets needs to be enhanced. Is this a system that needs fixing? Transmission is generally viewed as a classic example of a bottleneck market, where control of an essential transmission facility provides its owner with extraordinary market power. We argue that while bottleneck problems do occur in wholesale transmission, these markets often function rather well, and probably better than regulated retail markets.

In retail electric power markets, state regulators command an elaborate administrative process intended to protect consumers from a local utility's abuse of market power. This process is fortified by decades of legal precedent as to what constitute reasonable rates of return and prudent investments. Wholesale transactions nominally involve inter- state commerce, based in part on the difficulty of tracing the path of electrons. As such, they are outside the jurisdiction of state regulators and instead are regulated by the FERC. The official standard of FERC regulation is that firm wholesale transactions are priced at embedded costs and nonfirm transactions are priced on a split-the-savings basis, equal to the difference between the buyer's decremental cost and the seller's incremental cost. In practice, the FERC has in recent years provided considerable pricing flexibility in its approval of wholesale transactions (see Tenebaum and Henderson 1991).

It is a reasonable conclusion that FERC regulates wholesale transac- tions with a lighter hand than states regulate generation, transmission, and distribution at the retail level. It is also reasonable to expect that weak regulation by the FERC will risk abuses of market power. This will be evidenced by dispersion in wholesale prices, reflecting the extent of seller and buyer market power. In addition, wholesale market power might lead to inefficient utilization of generation and transmission re- sources. In what follows, we review evidence on the performance of wholesale markets as revealed by the operations of power pools and by price data on wholesale trades.[1]

Institutions currently exist to facilitate wholesale trades of electric power. The success of these institutions may serve as a measure of the need to promote competition in transmission. The most common of these institutions is the power pool, which can take several forms. In a "tight pool," existing units are dispatched centrally, meaning that a single operator adjusts unit outputs to meet demand at the lowest cost. Tight pools typically also have a formal structure for planning new investment and for establishing and enforcing reserve requirements. Table 1 lists the tight pools in the United States. Listed as a separate group in table 1 are utility holding companies, which generally organize production deci- sions centrally.

Most power pools, whether "tight" or otherwise, coordinate invest- ment plans and impose reserve requirements on their members. These

---

1. Another indicator of the performance of wholesale markets is the average level of prices. If, from a consumer perspective, wholesale regulation is less effective, wholesale prices will be higher than retail prices for utilities that generate their own power, after adjusting for relevant transmission and distribution costs. Although we have not made a systematic study of this relationship, there are several areas in the United States where this comparison would reveal much higher retail prices, despite more stringent regulation at the retail level.

requirements reflect the economies of joint operations and discourage free riding on the investments of other members. Pools differ in the extent to which this coordination is organized and enforced, and in the extent to which the pool acts centrally on behalf of its members.

Most of the centrally dispatched pools listed in table 1 also centralize the commitment of generating units to meet demand. Utilities "commit" a power plant by maintaining the plant in a status that is capable of delivering power on short notice. This usually requires that the plant be operating at light load (in a status as spinning reserve). Commitment is an important aspect of operations. Having too many plants in a standby status wastes resources; having too few plants reduces reliability. Among the centrally dispatched pools, all but the New York Power Pool centralize unit commitment. According to the 1989 FERC transmission task force report, centrally dispatched pools (including holding companies) accounted for about one-third of installed generating capacity in the United States in 1989.

Another variant of a power pool is the brokered pool. This is essentially a managed market for power. Brokered pools use auction markets or electronic bulletin boards to facilitate market transactions among their members. Typically, brokered pools do not engage in centralized dispatch or unit commitment. Examples of brokered pools include the Western Systems Power Pool (an experiment lasting from 1987 to 1989), the Mid-Continent Area Power Pool (MAPP), and the Florida pool.

The last category of power pools is the informal pool, which includes all pools that are not centrally dispatched or brokered. These pools vary considerably in degree of coordination, ranging from determined attempts to share resources to little more than a promise to facilitate operations in the event of an emergency.

TABLE 1.   Centrally Dispatched Power Pools in the United States

Michigan Electric Coordinating System
New England Power Pool
New York Power Pool
Pennsylvania-New Jersey-Maryland Interconnection

Allegheny Power System
American Electric Power Company
Middle South Utilities (Entergy)
The Southern Companies
Texas Utilities Company

Source: FERC 1989.

Power pools can enhance economic efficiency by coordinating investment decisions and by improving the utilization of existing capital. By sharing resources, a power pool allows its members to reduce the cost of preparedness for forced outages and to take advantage of noncoincident peak loads. A centrally dispatched pool only has to plan for the largest forced outage of all its members, while nonintegrated utilities have to maintain reserves that are large enough to cover the largest contingency at each firm. The pool may also benefit by producing to meet the demand of the pooled members, rather than meeting demand at each utility. To the extent that demands are not perfectly correlated, the load curve of the pool is likely to be flatter than the load curve for each of its members. This reduces the total maximum capacity that the member firms must maintain and increases resource utilization, so that the member firms can justify investment in a greater proportion of more efficient base and intermediate load generation plants.

Several factors discourage participation in highly coordinated power pools. Power pools interfere with a utility's freedom to make its own investment and dispatching decisions, and thus entail a loss of control. Management may be particularly opposed to loss of control if the utility has dominion over scarce resources that it can use to its own advantage, rather than share with a pool. Regulation discourages pool participation because the benefits of economy wholesale transactions are usually passed through to ratepayers. In addition, regulators may object to multijurisdictional pooling arrangements that could lead to conflicts or dilution of authority. A particular example is the sharing of risks from imprudent investments. Participation in a tightly organized pool could involve a sharing of some of these risks, which regulators would resist. One example is the conflict between Pennsylvania and New Jersey regulators over the cost consequences of the Three Mile Island accident. An economic obstacle to pooling is that it involves administration costs that may exceed the savings from increased coordination (see Palermo et al. 1990).[2]

Some insight into the operation of power pools may be obtained by examining statistics on wholesale trades. Table 2 shows the extent of wholesale trade, excluding requirements customers, as a fraction of retail sales for different regions. Some areas with strong pooling institutions, such as the Northeast (which has the New York and New England power pools) and ECAR (which has a number of holding companies), show a

---

2. In some cases, pooling may increase the risk of antitrust actions. For example, a tightly integrated pool that refuses to wheel power for a municipal customer may be a bigger target for antitrust action than a single, nonintegrated, utility.

TABLE 2.   Retail and Wholesale Sales, 1985

Region	Sales to Final Customers (MWh) (1)	Wholesale Sales Excluding Requirements Customers (MWh) (2)	Ratio (2)/(1)
Northeast (NYPP+NEPOOL)	224.7	79.2	35.2%
MAAC (Pa.-N.J.-Md. pool)	202.2	27.6	13.7
SERC	404.5	59.6	14.7
ECAR	382.0	129.6	33.9
SPP	202.2	34.3	17.0
ERCOT	179.8	3.1	1.7
MAIN	179.8	12.4	6.9
MAPP(brokered pool)	67.4	20.5	30.4
WSCC—North	157.3	103.9	66.1
WSCC—South	247.2	34.8	14.1
Total	2,247	505	22.5

Source: The data are reported in FERC 1989 and are derived from an unpublished report to the U.S. Department of Energy. A further complication is that Texas (ERCOT) is a self-contained transmission region that is not subject to FERC jurisdiction, so wholesale data on ERCOT are probably incomplete.

large incidence of wholesale trades. Yet other areas that are dominated by tight power pools show little wholesale trade, and some areas without tight power pools show a high proportion of wholesale transactions. The MAAC is dominated by the tight Pennsylvania-New Jersey-Maryland interconnection, but wholesale trades in this area are below the average for the entire country. The amount of wholesale trade is quite large in the Northwest, but the data in table 2 precede the adoption of the Western Systems Power Pool experiment in 1987, and so cannot be evidence for enhanced trade from formal pooling arrangements.

The extent of wholesale trade is an indirect and imprecise measure of the value of pooling. Some wholesale trades are merely wheeling transactions and are not associated with direct efficiency gains. Power may be transmitted across multiple utility jurisdictions through a series of buy-sell agreements, which presents the possibility that a transaction that is really only one trade will be counted as several wholesale trades. Conclusions as to the value of pooling institutions depend on further evidence on the efficiency of electricity production. This evidence may be derived from statistics relating to investment and capacity utilization under different pooling arrangements.[3]

---

3. Standard econometric cost function approaches to the value of pooling, such as Christensen and Greene 1978, have the difficulty that trade among utilities in the pool introduces additional variance and complicates estimation. Therefore, this study focuses on the actual experience of plant utilization by pooled and nonpooled utilities.

TABLE 3.   Pool Characteristics, 1989

	Total Number of Utilities	Mean Capacity (MW)	SD(MW)
1. Centrally dispatched pool	68	3,502	3,717
2. Brokered pool	63	2,547	4,143
3. Informal pool	27	2,028	1,886
4. No pool	61	2,993	5,839
5. Central and brokered pools	131	3,043	3,941
6. Informal and no pool	88	2,697	4,977

Note: Test of equality of mean generation capacities, group 5 vs. group 6: $t = 0.57$.

Data on Power Pools

The data used for this study cover 277 utilities. They include generation capacity, fuel source, type, heat rate, and operating costs for each plant owned by each utility in 1989, sales to end users, and power pool affiliation, if any, for each utility.[4] Table 3 shows some of the characteristics of the firms that make up the different power pool categories. Each category of power pool contains a large number of utilities of different sizes. Although the average generation capacity of centrally dispatched utilities exceeds the average capacity for utilities in other institutional arrangements, the differences are not statistically significant. The table reports the results of a statistical test for the equality of the mean capacities for group 5, which includes utilities that are in either central or brokered pools, and group 6, which includes utilities that are either in an informal pool or no pool at all. The low *t*-statistic indicates no statistically significant difference in the group means.

A benefit that a power pool can provide its members is the ability to satisfy the minimum requirements for system security with a lower generation reserve margin than the members would need if they did not pool their resources. Define the reserve margin of utility i by

$$R_i = \frac{(K_i - D_i)}{D_i},$$

---

4. Plant-level data are drawn primarily from FERC Form 1 and U.S. Energy Information Administration (EIA) Form 861 reports. Other utility-level data were obtained from various EIA publications listed in the references (U.S. Department of Energy 1991a–f).

where K_i is the total installed capacity and D_i is the peak demand, measured by sales to end users.[5] For utilities that are members of a power pool, represented by p, define the aggregate reserve margin of the pool as

$$R_p = \frac{K_p - D_p}{D_p} , \tag{1}$$

where $K_p = \Sigma_{i \in p} K_i$, the total installed capacity of the pool, and $D_p = \Sigma_{i \in p} D_i$, the sum of the pool members' noncoincident peak demands. As discussed previously, pooled utilities may be able to maintain a lower aggregate reserve margin because pooling makes the members' single largest contingency a smaller fraction of total demand, or because with diverse loads the peak demand of the pool is less than the sum of the peak demands of its members. This does not mean, of course, that each utility in the pool will have a lower reserve margin than it would maintain if it were not in the pool. Some utilities may invest in excess capacity with the intention of sharing capacity with other, generation-deficient, members.

As a test of the hypothesis that pooling may allow members to hold fewer excess reserves, we compare the aggregate reserve margins of pooled utilities with the aggregate reserve margins of utilities that are not pooled. The latter is defined by

$$R_{np} = \sum_{i \in np} \frac{K_i - D_i}{D_i} \cdot \frac{D_i}{D_{np}} = \frac{K_{np} - D_{np}}{D_{np}} , \tag{2}$$

where K_{np} is the total capacity of all utilities that are not pooled and D_{np} is the sum of their noncoincident demands. The aggregate reserve margin is the weighted average reserve margin for all nonpooled utilities, with the weights given by each utility's share of the total noncoincident peak demand. As equation 2 shows, this is consistent with the definition of the aggregate reserve margin of pooled utilities given in equation 1, with K_{np} and D_{np} replacing K_p and D_p.

Table 4 shows the aggregate reserve margins for each class of coordinating institution. These aggregate reserve margins are defined as in equations 1 and 2, except that the pooled utilities are partitioned by class of pooling institution. The table shows a significant variation in aggregate margins across the different pooling institutions. Utilities that are not associated with a formal power pool had an aggregate reserve

---

5. Data on firm capacities and peak demands are from Electrical World 1991.

margin in 1989 that was almost twice as large as the aggregate reserve margin for utilities in centrally dispatched pools.

If the differences in the means in table 4 are statistically significant, this would be evidence that pooling promotes efficient investment in generation capacity, assuming that the lower reserve margins in table 4 do not compromise system reliability. Of course the differences in the aggregate margins in table 4 could be explained by factors other than improved coordination. Figure 1 is a scatter plot of individual utility reserve margins as a function of installed capacity. The diagram shows that there is no meaningful relation between average reserve margin and capacity. This and the earlier result that average capacities are not statistically different for each class of pooling institution lend support to a conclusion that aggregate reserve margins are not primarily a consequence of differences in utility sizes in each coordination class.

TABLE 4.   Aggregate Reserve Margins, 1989

1. Centrally dispatched pool	13.5%
2. Brokered pool	15.8
3. Informal pool	9.6
4. No pool	24.0
5. Central and brokered pools	14.4
6. Informal and no pool	20.3

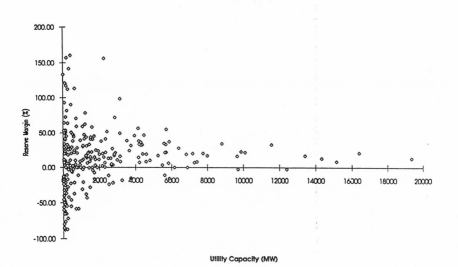

Fig. 1. Utility reserve margins vs. capacity

TABLE 5.   Test of Significance of Power Pooling

$R_i = C + \beta_1 I_{1i} + \beta_2 I_{2i} + \beta_3 I_{3i} + \epsilon_i$ $\epsilon_i \sim N(0, \sigma^2/K_i)$			
Variable	Coeff.	St. Error	t-Statistic
C	27.6	2.9	9.46
I_1	−9.8	3.9	−2.53
I_2	−7.1	4.3	−1.67
I_3	−11.1	6.1	−1.82

Note: R_i = reserve margin of utility *i*; I_1 = centrally dispatched pool; I_2 = brokered pool; I_3 = informal pool.

It is evident from figure 1 that utility reserve margins are heteroskedastic. This should be expected. The minimum efficient base load plant size (while decreasing in recent years) was about 500 MW in this relevant time period. The data include many small utilities for which planning errors, given minimum efficient scale, are likely to be very large. In order to test the significance of differences in aggregate reserve margins for the different pooling institutions, we corrected for heteroskedasticity by dividing sample variances by the utility's installed capacity. With this adjustment, table 5 shows that pooling is associated with a statistically significant difference in reserve margins. Note, however, that the results in table 5 are not strictly comparable to the aggregate reserve margins shown in table 4. The reserve margins in table 4 are the aggregate reserve margins for the entire pool category. The reserve margin data used in the regression reported in table 5 are individual utility reserve margins unweighted by demand shares.[6]

The populations of pooled and nonpooled utilities differ in their distributions of reserve margins. Figure 2 is a scatter diagram of reserve margins for utilities in centrally dispatched pools and brokered pools. Figure 3 shows the same for utilities in either informal pools or in nonpooled firms. The scatter plots show that both groups include both small and large firms, although the informal/no pool category has more firms that are very small. Municipal utilities are disproportionately represented in the nonpooled category. Municipalities often concentrate their investments in local distribution and purchase power from others. This would contribute to low (possibly negative) reserve margins calculated on a base of owned capacity for these firms. Many of the informal pools

6. If the reserve margins used in the regression analysis were weighted by demand shares, then the average in each category of pooling institution would be the aggregate reserve margin reported in table 4. However, this would complicate the statistical test for equality of means.

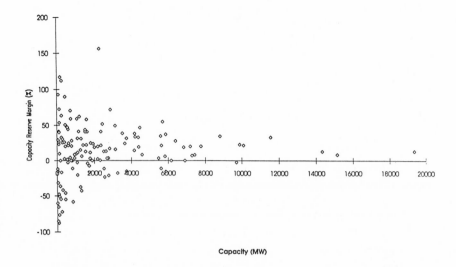

Fig. 2. Reserve margins vs. capacity, centrally dispatched, and broker-pooled firms

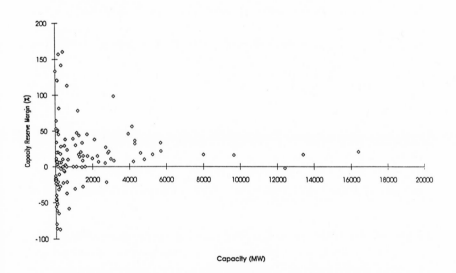

Fig. 3. Reserve margins vs. capacity, informal pool, and nonpooled firms

TABLE 6.   Capacity Utilization of Base Load Plants, 1989

	Average Plant Utilization
1. Centrally dispatched pool	56.6%
2. Brokered pool	54.4
3. Informal pool	55.8
4. No pool	51.7
5. Centrally dispatched and brokered pools	55.7
6. Informal and no pool	52.9

are in the western United States, where municipal utilities have access to power from federal hydroelectric projects. This could be a partial explanation for the low aggregate reserve margin for this group.

Our results are consistent with the theory that pooling allows utilities to operate with lower reserve margins by improving the coordination of investment decisions, although the evidence is not overwhelming. Lower reserve margins have a large impact on total cost and will enhance economic efficiency provided that they do not compromise reliability. Improving investment is arguably the most important function of wholesale coordination,[7] however benefits from pooling may also be found in the utilization of existing resources. Benefits from coordination are realized if, accounting for transmission constraints, the marginal costs of generation for different utilities are approximately equal at each point in time. Any differences in marginal cost will allow gains from trade, assuming that power can be exchanged without serious transmission constraints or losses. Unfortunately, data are not readily available to test the hypothesis of equal marginal costs. Instead, we can ask whether pooled utilities are better, on average, in the utilization of their existing resources.

A test for efficiency in resource utilization is whether base load capacity utilization (which has the lowest incremental cost) is higher for pooled utilities, and whether peaking capacity is lower. It is conceivable that utilities that do not belong to a coordinated pool will have fewer opportunities to sell production from excess base load capacity or to purchase power from others instead of relying on their own high-cost peaking capacity. However, any meaningful comparison of capacity utilization across different pooling institutions needs to be adjusted for the different demand and supply conditions that face each firm.

Table 6 shows average capacity utilization of base load plants by

---

7. According to a FERC study of power pooling, "The greatest economy potentials of interconnection, coordination and pooling lie in the ability to achieve the economies of scale through construction of large generating units and reduction of reserve margins" (1981, 166).

pooling institution. The differences (e.g., between pooling categories 5 and 6) are statistically significant, suggesting that strong pooling institutions are more effective in utilizing their members' least-cost resources. However, the numbers in table 6 do not account for the previous observation that utilities that do not pool have higher reserve margins. A higher reserve margin means that, ceteris paribus, the firm has a large supply of capacity relative to demand. As a consequence, the utilization of the firm's base load capacity may be limited by inadequate demand for production from these resources.

To adjust for the impact of demand on base load capacity utilization, we have constructed an index that is the expected percentage of base load utilization for each pool classification under the assumptions that all base load capacity is equally efficient and that the demand for electricity at each utility is normally distributed over time. The appendix describes the calculation and use of this index in some detail. The point of this index is to normalize base load capacity according to the fraction of the year in which it may be used. Table 7 shows the unadjusted base load utilization numbers, the indices, and the ratio of the unadjusted utilization to the index. The latter is likely to be a more accurate measure of the extent to which utilities utilize their base load capacity after adjusting for different levels of capacity and demand.

The numbers in the last column of table 7 are the ratios of the unadjusted base load capacity utilization from table 6 to the calculated demand index for the utilities in each pooling category. These ratios are an estimate of normalized base load capacity utilization. The results in table 7 show that base load capacity utilization is *higher* for utilities that do not pool, *after adjusting for their higher reserve margins.* Therefore, one cannot conclude that pooling institutions allow utilities to make better use of their most efficient resources. If anything, it would appear that those

TABLE 7. Capacity Utilization of Base Load Plants, 1989

| | Average Plant Utilization | | |
	No Capacity Adjustment (a)	Demand Index (b)	Ratio (a)/(b)
1. Centrally dispatched pool	56.6%	57.9%	1.0
2. Brokered pool	54.4	53.2	1.0
3. Informal pool	55.8	65.1	0.9
4. No pool	51.7	42.8	1.2
5. Centrally dispatched and brokered pools	55.7	55.8	1.0
6. Informal and no pool	52.9	48.2	1.1

TABLE 8.   Capacity and Utilization of Peaking Plants, 1989

	Peaking as Percentage of Installed Capacity	Utilization of Peaking Capacity
1. Centrally dispatched pool	14.8%	3.3%
2. Brokered pool	18.2	2.8
3. Informal pool	15.7	0.5
4. No pool	16.3	2.4
5. Centrally dispatched and brokered pools	15.9	3.1
6. Informal and no pool	16.1	1.8

utilities that do not pool have been particularly successful in making arrangements to sell their excess base load capacity to others. This conclusion is tempered by the admittedly imprecise adjustment for demand conditions, but the adjustment is at least sufficient to question any enhanced base load operating efficiencies from pooling.

If pooling does not affect the utilization of utilities' most efficient resources, might it still be beneficial in economizing on the use of less efficient resources? This could come about in two ways. First, if pooling improves a firm's load duration curve (makes the load duration curve flatter), then utilities that pool will not have to install as much peaking capacity.[8] Second, assuming the same amounts and composition of generating capacity and the same peak demand, a flatter load duration curve will lead to increased utilization of peaking capacity by pooling utilities. These possibilities are investigated in table 8.

The first column in table 8 shows that there is essentially no difference between the percentage of peaking capacity that utilities install, based on their participation in power pools (the differences are not statistically significant). Pooled utilities tend to have a higher utilization of peaking capacity. However, this is almost certainly a result of the fact that pooled utilities tend to have lower reserve margins, which result in a higher rate of capacity utilization for all of their resources.

This review of the effects of power pooling institutions shows little evidence that power pooling has a discernible impact on the utilization of *existing* utility resources. A possible explanation for this result is that resource utilization is almost entirely determined by a utility's native supply and demand and is not significantly affected by wholesale transactions. This explanation is unlikely to be correct. Table 2 shows that many utilities are dependent on wholesale transactions, and there is much

---

8. Peaking capacity is defined as all oil or natural gas combustion turbine capacity.

anecdotal evidence that utilities benefit enormously from opportunities to engage in wholesale trade. A more likely explanation is that utilities are able to capture many of the benefits of integration without formal institutions; power pools have little additional effect in promoting wholesale trade. Utilities appear to do rather well on their own in conducting wholesale market operations, whether or not they are members of closely integrated power pools.

Does Efficient Utilization Mean Absence of Market Power?

Efficient capacity utilization is not sufficient to prove that there is no significant market power in wholesale trades. Utilities may accommodate existing resources, yet refuse to grant the firm long-term transmission access that is needed to risk investment in new generation facilities. Resources may be used efficiently, but the rents from those resources may go disproportionately to the owners of transmission assets. An example is a perfectly discriminating monopsonist. The exercise of monopsony power (e.g., by lowering the purchase price for power after a plant is built) would discourage investment in new capacity whose output is intended to be sold to buyers who have market power. Our results showing that pooled utilities have lower reserve margins neither reject nor support a finding of wholesale market power. Utilities that participate in highly coordinated pools may be less concerned about opportunistic behavior in wholesale purchases and sales, either because they have adopted rules to mitigate strategic behavior or because they have developed long-term relationships that discourage opportunism. These firms may be more willing to invest based on the reserve requirements of the pool, rather than on their own needs, and this will be reflected in more efficient (lower) reserve margins. In transactions that are external to the power pool, opportunistic behavior may still be a threat to the development of wholesale trade.

Partial evidence on the ability of transmission owners to collect rents can be obtained from a study of wholesale transactions in the West. The western transmission market appears approximately as shown in figure 4. The main transmission lines are the northwest DC and AC interties and the lines leading to Southern California from the Southwest.

Sales of firm energy are based on embedded production costs, and so are largely unrelated to competitive conditions (although the FERC has been somewhat more relaxed about this requirement in recent years). Sales of nonfirm energy are based on sellers' incremental costs and buyers' decremental costs, and so should reflect competitive conditions.

Table 9 shows sales and average prices of nonfirm wholesale energy in the years 1985 and 1988 for what is termed the Northwest and the Southwest (sub)markets. The Southwest market is the shaded area in figure 4. The remainder is the Northwest market, except that California utilities with significant transmission holdings are assumed to participate in both markets.

Nonfirm energy in the Northwest is dominated by surplus hydropower. In the Southwest, nonfirm energy is predominately surplus coal generation. Utilities in each of these markets are reasonably interconnected with other utilities in the same market, but interconnections

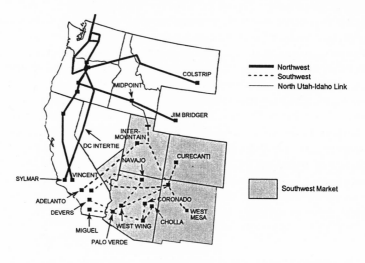

Fig. 4. Major transmission routes from the northwest and southwest

TABLE 9.   Sales and Average Prices of Nonfirm
Energy

	Sales (GWh)	Average Price ($/MWh)
1985		
Northwest	43,767	19.9
Southwest	18,190	26.6
1988		
Northwest	18,312	18.3
Southwest	16,479	18.7

between the two markets are limited. The exceptions are the California utilities that have entitlements on both the main north-to-south and east-to-west transmission systems (mainly Southern California Edison).

If there were no market power in transmission, one would expect prices for nonfirm energy to be about the same in both markets. This was approximately the case in 1988, but not in 1985. Many factors determine the demand and supply for nonfirm energy, including Bonneville Power, which controls crucial transmission capacity from British Columbia into the western states. Two events figure prominently in the change in relative prices from 1985 to 1988. Oil and gas prices fell from 1985 to 1988. This had a direct negative impact on buyers' decremental costs, and hence their willingness to pay for economy energy. Although most surplus energy in the Southwest is coal fired, lower oil and gas prices put downward competitive pressure on the price of surplus coal (Joskow 1990). Also in 1988, a dry year reduced the supply of hydropower in the Northwest. Thus, arbitrage between these two markets tended to close the gap between nonfirm energy prices in the Southwest and the Northwest in 1988. In 1985, fossil fuel prices were higher and hydropower was in more plentiful supply. As a result, there was a greater scope for buyers to exercise their market power in purchase of hydropower from the Northwest, and arbitrage of these markets was not profit maximizing. Note that while buyers could exercise market power in the purchase of hydropower, other actors, such as Bonneville Power, have seller-market power and can act to keep the price of hydropower above its competitive level, so the outcome of this bargaining is not easy to predict.

Conclusions and Policy Recommendations

The Energy Policy Act of 1992 gives the FERC broad powers to mandate access to transmission for wholesale transactions. If the FERC were to exercise these powers, it would turn the U.S. transmission grid into a system of privately owned common carriers. Whether such open access would contribute to significant improvements in the efficiency of the wholesale electric power market is questionable. Using data on utility plants and participation in power pools, we have argued that membership in various coordination institutions has not led to substantial improvements in the efficiency of utility operations. If utilities are impeded in their access to wholesale suppliers and buyers, the existence of institutions that are designed to facilitate access (such as centrally coordinated power pools) should lead to observable improvements in operating efficiencies. We see some evidence that utilities that participate in formal pools are able to sustain lower reserve margins. However, this evidence is weak, and there is no support for the conclusion that these utilities are more efficient in the utilization of their generating resources.

We acknowledge that evidence on the utilization of existing assets is not sufficient to determine whether market power at the wholesale level is a deterrent to new investment. Data on trades in the West suggest that there is wholesale market power, which is revealed by large price differences for nonfirm energy between contiguous geographical submarkets. The opportunity for utilities to exercise monopsony power through ownership of transmission resources could be a major threat to the viability of new nonutility wholesale suppliers. This is a primary motivation for the empowerment of the FERC to mandate access. Yet our results underscore the need for regulators to appreciate the efficiencies of the present wholesale market, particularly for nonfirm transactions, when designing policies to correct alleged market failures.

APPENDIX

The demand index numbers used in table 7 indicate the expected energy produced by base load resources as a fraction of total energy produced, calculated separately for each utility. This appendix details the algorithm used to calculate these index numbers.

Available data provide the annual peak demand (in MW) and annual total demand (in MWh) for each utility. As a fraction of peak demand, expected hourly demand is a utility's load factor: LF = average demand / peak demand, where average demand is total annual demand divided by 8,760 hours per year. We assume peak demand is a certain number, r, of standard deviations above average demand, so that the standard deviation of demand can be calculated as $\sigma = (1 - LF) / r$. A value of $r = 3.1$ is common (Lawrence Berkeley Laboratory 1984) and is used in the calculations.

With the assumption of normally distributed demand, the cumulative distribution function of demand is

$$cnorm(z(x)) \equiv \int_0^{z(x)} \frac{1}{\sqrt{2\pi}} \exp\left(\frac{-t^2}{2}\right) dt,$$

where x is hourly demand as a fraction of peak demand, and $z(x)$ is the statistic $z(x) = (x - LF) / \sigma$.

To calculate the demand index number for a utility, we use the cumulative distribution function of demand to calculate the expected utilization rate of capacity classified as base load. This utilization rate is the expected total output of all base load plants divided by the maximum potential supply from those plants.

Base load capacity is assumed to service the first $\alpha \times 100\%$ of peak demand, where α = total capacity classified as base load (in MW) divided by total utility capacity (in MW). By construction, the area beneath $1 - cnorm(z(x))$ from $x = 0$ to 1 represents expected demand, as a fraction of the peak; the area beneath this function from $x = 0$ to α represents expected hourly production from only base load units, again expressed as a fraction of the peak. Denoting this latter region as β, the utilization rate is therefore

$$\frac{\text{expected output}}{\text{maximum potential output}} = \frac{\beta \times (\text{peak demand}) \times 8{,}760 \text{ MWh/year}}{\alpha \times (\text{peak demand}) \times 8{,}760 \text{ MWh/year}}$$

and the demand index number for a utility with demand distribution $cnorm(z(x))$ is

$$\text{Demand Index} = \frac{1}{\alpha} \int_0^\alpha [1 - cnorm(z(x))] \, dx.$$

The load duration curve is a transformation of the distribution of demand that provides the percent of time actual demand exceeds each possible level of demand. The usual graph of the load duration curve plots demand x on the ordinate and Prob $\{X > x\} = 1 - cnorm(z(x))$ on the abscissa. Therefore, the demand index number (expected utilization rate of base load capacity) is equivalent to the area beneath the load duration curve serviced by base load capacity relative to the total energy potentially available from all base load plants.

REFERENCES

Baldick, R., and E. Kahn. 1993. "Network Costs and the Regulation of Wholesale Competition in Electric Power." *Journal of Regulatory Economics* 5, no. 4: 367–84.

Baron, D., and R. Myerson. 1982. "Regulating a Monopolist with Unknown Costs." *Econometrica* 50: 911–30.

Christensen, L., and W. Greene. 1978. "An Econometric Assessment of Cost Savings from Coordination in United States Electric Power Generation." *Land Economics* 54: 139–55.

Electrical World. 1991. *Directory of Electric Utilities*. New York: McGraw-Hill.

Federal Energy Regulatory Commission (FERC). 1981. *Power Pooling in the United States*. Washington, D.C.: FERC-0049.

Federal Energy Regulatory Commission (FERC). 1989. *Transmission Task Force's Report to the Commission. Electricity Transmission: Realities, Theory and Policy Alternatives*. October.

Gilbert, R., and M. Riordan. 1992. "Regulating Complementary Products: A Problem of Institutional Choice." Working Paper. University of California, Berkeley.

Joskow, P. 1990. "The Performance of Long-Term Contracts: Further Evidence from Coal Markets." *Rand Journal of Economics* 21: 251–74.

Jurewitz, J. 1993. "Life After the Energy Policy Act." *The Electricity Journal* 6, no. 5: 48–65.

Laffont, J.-J., and J. Tirole. 1993. *A Theory of Incentives in Procurement and Regulation*. Cambridge: MIT Press.

Lawrence Berkeley Laboratory. 1984. "Financial Impacts on Utilities of Load Shape Changes Project: Stage I Technical Report." LBL-19750, Energy Analysis Program, Applied Science Division.

Otter Tail Power Co. v United States. 1973. 410 US 366.

Palermo, P. J., J. A. Casazza, D. J. LeKang, and H. D. Limmer. 1990. "The UCIX Experiment: An Evaluation of 1989." Working Paper. Arlington, VA: Casazza, Schultz and Associates.

Schmalensee, R., and B. Golub. 1984. "Estimating Effective Concentration in Deregulated Wholesale Electricity Markets." *Rand Journal of Economics*. 12 (Spring): 26

Tenebaum, B.,and S. Henderson. 1991. "Market Based Pricing of Wholesale Electric Services." *Electricity Journal* 4, no. 10: 30–45.

U.S. Department of Energy (DOE). 1991a. *Electric Plant Cost and Power Production Expenses 1989*. Washington, D.C.: Energy Information Administration, DOE/EIA-0455.

U.S. Department of Energy (DOE). 1991b. *Inventory of Power Plants in the United States 1989*. Washington, D.C.: Energy Information Administration, DOE/EIA-0095.

U.S. Department of Energy (DOE). 1991c. *Electric Power Annual 1989*. Washington, D.C.: Energy Information Administration, DOE/EIA-0348.

U.S. Department of Energy (DOE). 1991d. *Electric Sales and Revenue 1989*. Washington, D.C.: Energy Information Administration, DOE/EIA-0540.

U.S. Department of Energy (DOE). 1991e. *Financial Statistics of Selected Investor-Owned Electric Utilities 1989*. Washington, D.C.: Energy Information Administration, DOE/EIA-0437/1.

U.S. Department of Energy (DOE). 1991f. *Financial Statistics of Selected Investor-Owned Electric Utilities 1989*. Washington, D.C.: Energy Information Administration, DOE/EIA-0437/2.

Part 2

Introduction to Part 2: Analyzing Public Utilities as Infrastructure in a Holistic Setting—The New Challenge for Public Policy

Harry M. Trebing

Public utilities have always been viewed as social overhead capital and therefore an integral part of a nation's infrastructure. However, in the past, most attention focused on the economic regulation of utilities and carriers, with little consideration given to their roles as comprehensive networks supplying electricity, gas, telecommunications, and water. Only recently has attention shifted toward an examination of public utilities as elaborate systems of supply that incorporate comprehensive transmission and distribution networks. This change in emphasis introduces new dimensions of efficiency and performance,[1] as well as a host of new issues dealing with network access, network pricing, monopoly focal points, interconnection criteria, and the boundaries between suppliers of service, consumers, and networks as infrastructure.

This introduction will examine network characteristics and inherent economies. However, attainment of these economies cannot be divorced from the broader setting in which the strategies of management, the behavior of user groups, and the shortcomings of both markets and government regulation affect the realization of such economies. The role and influence of these factors are important if the resources committed to the provision of utility services are to be employed efficiently and the potential gains inherent in the interdependent relationship between infrastructure investment on the one hand, and growth in productivity and real income on the other are to be realized.

---

1. As an example, see Robin Mansell, *The New Telecommunications: A Political Economy of Network Evolution* (London: Sage Publications, 1993).

Fundamental Network Characteristics and Economies

There are at least 10 distinctive features of energy and telecommunication networks. First, networks involve heavy capital investments because of the need to connect all subscribers in a service territory. Second, networks have significant common and joint costs that result in economies of scope and economies of joint production in the provision of multiple services. Third, there may be economies of scale associated with building a large network in advance of demand. However, the consequences of failing to forecast future patterns of demand correctly can make such advance planning precarious. Fourth, the more segments there are in a network, the greater the amount of traffic that will be handled by an individual segment, other things being equal. As a corollary, each additional segment will tend to increase traffic on other segments of that network. Fifth, networks provide inexpensive backup capacity through interconnection with alternative sources of supply. This may take the form of routing alternatives, pooled reserves, or simply spreading the risk of outages or failures over a larger universe. Sixth, networks will reduce the need for capacity to meet peak demand regardless of outages or failures. This will be accomplished by incorporating a number of individual coincident system peaks within a larger framework so that they are converted into noncoincident peaks, thereby improving the system's overall diversity factor. Seventh, advances in software permit a network to achieve greater flexibility in serving different classes of customers over a common facility. This is particularly evident in telecommunications, where software permits a network to handle complex mixtures of voice, video, and data traffic with increasing flexibility through dynamic bandwidth management. Comparable gains in network functionality from the use of software can also be expected in electricity and natural gas networks. Paradoxically, while the use of software enhances functionality, it also serves to increase overhead costs for the network. In fact, for a facility-based telecommunication carrier, the cost of network design and software is reputedly greater than the cost of laying fiber. Eighth, network size and technological change interact to permit the adoption of new methods for packaging and transmitting service. This is clearly evident in telecommunications, where progressively greater blocks of data can be moved much more rapidly as a result of the introduction of packet switching and the coming change to cell relay and asynchronous transfer mode (ATM) technology. Similar advances can be expected in the transportation of power and natural gas. Ninth, the incremental cost of offering special services to individual classes of customers diminishes as the size of the network increases. This is clearly discernible in telecommunications, where the incremental cost of supplying custom network offerings or virtual private networks to large users diminishes with system size. Tenth, there are obvious externalities when an increase in the number of persons using a network enhances its value to an individual user, but there are at least three other significant spillover effects. Networks have the potential for controlling social costs and negative externalities by permitting the environmental dispatch of electricity. Networks can also increase the options of buyers, thereby eroding the market power of individual suppliers. For example, a comprehensive interstate pipeline network would diminish the market power associated with a high concentration of proved reserves among a few major oil and gas producers in a given field by giving buyers access to many more fields. Finally, telecommunication networks can expand the size of the market available to sellers and thereby contribute to a greater division of labor and a consequent increase in productivity.

At this point it is important to note one significant difference between telecommunication networks and electric and gas networks. For telecommunications, new technology has caused a proliferation of alternative delivery systems. These systems may be based on a variety of wireless, landline, and satellite technologies, but it is by no means clear that alternative delivery systems are always close substitutes for one another. Rather, these systems appear to have a strong complementary relationship based on comparative advantage in terms of cost, reliability, and quality of service. The problem, of course, is how to assure that consumers can combine or choose between different delivery systems in a fashion that best satisfies their needs. This will involve internetwork coordination at a level that far surpasses current interconnection and unbundling proposals if a network of networks that minimizes transactions costs is to be achieved.

Barriers to Network Efficiency

The network characteristics previously described can give rise to unique problem areas that will affect the realization of network economies. Three areas deserve special attention: (1) the propensity toward high market concentration, (2) the conflict between decentralized access and centralized network management, and (3) the impact of perverse public policies.

The cumulative effect of network characteristics will tend to result in large systems relative to the size of a given market. To the extent that the incumbent firm providing the network must have a major share of the market to be successful, high levels of concentration will prevail and new entrants will be at a distinct disadvantage. When minimum efficient market share is greater than 50 percent, the implications for direct competition are obvious. Furthermore, large sunk cost investment in networks will serve as a barrier to entry and negate the applicability of potential entry or contestable market theory.[2] New entrants will also have to cope with the long gestation period needed to achieve financial viability. For example, it took MCI more than 10 years to earn an adequate rate of return, and for a number of years capital markets attached a zero or negative value to United Telephone's investment in Sprint. Again, the implications for further entry into the long-distance market by facility-based carriers are clear. Finally, the need to achieve high load and capacity factors provides a strong stimulus for network pricing that seeks to exploit opportunities for price discrimination and cross-subsidization. The fact that networks serve highly differentiated markets of differing demand elasticities facilitates these pricing strategies. Furthermore, the incentive to engage in such pricing applies not only to the existing network, but also to expansion of the network and to modernization.

On balance, network characteristics will tend to prescribe industry structures that are inherently concentrated. Such concentration is conducive to market dominance, which, in turn, provides both the incentive and the latitude for employing anticompetitive strategies. Hence, structures, market dominance, and behavior interact to reinforce concentration and circumscribe pervasive competition.

Another area of concern is the potential conflict between promoting open access and the unbundling of capacity and service and, the effective management of the network. The natural gas transmission network provides an example. Pipeline networks with multiple pickup and delivery points require centralized dispatch, control of supply, flow routing, and storage scheduling. Open access and independent decisions by buyers and sellers of gas can reduce the system manager's options for dispatching gas and balancing the system. Furthermore, capacity entitlements will depend on how much gas is being taken at other locations, so that neither the pipeline nor the customers of unbundled services can determine availability without knowing what other customers will use at other points. Improperly handled, free access can actually reduce the total capacity of a network. Whether improved network functionality,

---

2. Potential entry will be meaningful only when the new entrant can realize all inherent network economies at a minimum efficient market share that will still assure a low Herfindahl-Hirshman Index (e.g., .20) or a Landes-Posner Index significantly below .50. It is possible that a drastic change in technology could distort these measures, but then only on the assumption that the new technology is not available to all firms.

especially using new advances in software, can correct this type of trans-actions cost remains to be seen.

Finally, there is the prospect that network economies may be ne-gated by public policies that promote duplication and redundancy. Such forms of public policy failure will primarily arise when government seeks to artificially stimulate entry, allocate markets between rivals, and as-sure service that will not otherwise be maintained. For example, the Federal Energy Regulatory Commission (FERC) attempted to encour-age new pipeline construction through optional certification and other forms of liberalized licensing, but the outcome was to create excess capacity in the industry.[3] As a consequence of FERC's adoption of the straight fixed variable costing methodology (SFV) in Order 636 (1992), much of the cost of this redundancy will be shifted forward to those consumers whose demand is most inelastic. Under SFV, fixed costs are assessed against those who use gas during the peak period. In practice, this means that such costs will fall primarily on residential and small business customers, who do not have the ability to switch to alternative sources of fuel during winter months. In telecommunications, the pros-pect that duplication and excess capacity will negate network economies is less obvious because the introduction of fiber and digital switching tends to dramatically lower costs. However, a question can still be raised as to whether bypass of local exchanges by fiber rings or the duplication of plant inherent in the rivalry between cable carriers and local exchange carriers results in excess capacity that will eventually burden residual customers with the fewest alternatives.

A Preface to Reform

The interaction of market failure and flawed public policies can consti-tute a significant obstacle to the attainment of network economies. As might be expected, numerous proposals for reform have been offered, but it is important to recognize that the success of any reform will depend upon its ability to treat three structural features that would appear to typify the public utility industries for the foreseeable future.

The first is the persistence of basic service or core markets for which there are few realistic alternative sources of supply. In fact, these basic service markets may not erode significantly over time. As consumer requirements grow in sophistication as a result of the infor-

---

3. For further discussion, see Paula G. Rosput, "The Limits to Deregulation of Entry and Expansion of the U.S. Gas Pipeline Industry," *Utilities Policy* 3, no. 4 (October 1993): 287–97.

mation revolution and broadened forms of energy utilization, the demand for reliable basic service (and therefore the vulnerability of these markets to exploitative pricing) may actually increase. It might be argued that the emergence of tight oligopoly instead of single-firm monopoly will diminish this threat, but this would only mean that the form of exploitative pricing has changed. Price leadership, limit entry pricing, conscious parallelism, and price caps that do not compel experimentation with lower prices cannot be viewed as significant advances over traditional first-, second-, and third-degree price discrimination applied by a monopolist under rate-of-return regulation. The potential for price discrimination, cross-subsidization, and risk shifting remains; the application only becomes more difficult to detect.

Of course, it can be argued that captive markets will disappear in the face of independent marketers and brokers who can resell the service—particularly electricity and natural gas. Such suppliers, however, are vulnerable to a vertical squeeze since they are dependent on the facility-based utility for capacity and must compete with the same firm in retail sales. There is also the question of reliability during periods of constrained supply, since brokers and marketers typically deal in short-term contracts. In telecommunications, brokers and resellers appear to serve niche, specialty markets rather than basic service customers.

A second factor is the continuing ability of large buyers to extract price and service concessions from utilities and carriers. The result of such bargaining will be to drive down the prices paid by monopsonists and raise prices paid by all other classes of customers. The distributional consequences of this type of behavior are clear. What is more difficult to detect are the allocative consequences of networks whose design reflects concessions to monopsonistic buyers. This may be particularly important in telecommunications, where network modernization appears to be driven by the requirements of the large user (or multinational firm), while basic service users are compelled to make payments for new plant for which they are not causally responsible. Again, it does not appear that monopsony power will be eroded in the foreseeable future. In fact, unbundling will strengthen the bargaining position of such buyers in an oligopolistic setting. This serves to explain why large buyers have been aggressive proponents of deregulation.

A third factor is the massive movement on the part of telecommunication, electric, and natural gas utilities toward programs that place much of the activity of the firm beyond the scope of regulation. This can be accomplished through diversification into unregulated markets, expansion into foreign markets, or the redefinition of regulatory boundaries to exclude specific activities of the enterprise. The objective is to enhance overall earnings and exploit operational and financial synergisms. Evidence of entry into overseas markets has been particularly strong in the wake of foreign privatization programs. For example, by 1993, 20 large electric and gas companies had 73 programs in 32 foreign countries, while the 9 largest U.S. telephone carriers (excluding AT&T and MCI) had 265 programs in 52 foreign countries.[4]

Given the magnitude of diversification and overseas investment, there is a distinct possibility that such activity may lead to denigration of the domestic network through disinvestment, failure to innovate, or deferred maintenance. Recent studies suggest that this is a legitimate concern. For example, Economics and Technology, Inc. compared new net plant investment with depreciation charges on an annual basis for regional Bell companies and found evidence of net disinvestment.[5] Quality of service may also be adversely affected by the shift from rate-of-return to price cap regulation. As Kwoka notes, rate-of-return regulation may not foster high-quality service, but it also does not reward low quality. The shift to price caps, on the other hand, "strengthens the incentive to underprovide quality."[6] The traditional remedy for this problem would be to raise the allowed rate of return for domestic network facilities to stimulate new investment and modernization. However, risk/return relationships can be distorted by the artificial stimulus inherent in the consolidation of utility and venture capital in a single holding company, resulting in an understatement of the required return for new investments in nonregulated activities. Similarly, there may be an overestimation of the gains from synergism and an underestimation of the risks of foreign investment. The implications for maintaining network performance are clear. There must be regulatory monitoring of quality of service and infrastructure investment, and oversight to prevent the burden of any failure of conglomerate diversification from being shifted to core/basic service markets.

A Critique of Two Options for Enhancing Network Performance

The proliferation of proposed reforms designed to improve efficiency can be placed in two broad categories. The first involves open entry to

---

4. For an extensive survey of foreign investment programs by U.S. telephone, electric, and gas utility holding companies, see C. D. Wasden, *A Descriptive Compendium of the International Activities of Major U.S.-Based Utility Holding Companies* (Columbus: National Regulatory Research Institute, June 1993).

5. See ETI Research Report, *Patterns of Investment by the Regional Bell Holding Companies* (Boston: Economics and Technology, Inc., May 1993).

6. See John E. Kwoka, "Implementing Price Caps in Telecommunications" *Journal of Policy Analysis and Management* 12, no. 4 (1993): 733.

the network and "light' regulation of individual services. An early example was the Public Service of Indiana Proposal (1991), whereby PSI would offer open access to its transmission and distribution network in exchange for freedom to set demand-based rates for electricity. The assumption was that any effort to charge extortionist prices would encourage the importation of outside power. A proposal by Ameritech (1993) offered open access to its telecommunication network in return for abandonment of rate-of-return regulation, freedom to enter interLATA markets, and greater pricing flexibility. Light regulation would take the form of price caps for selected services on an interim basis. Open access to the network was also embodied in the Federal Communications Commission's concept of open network architecture, which was combined with price caps (1991) for the regional Bell operating companies. In none of these proposals was there an intent to restructure the firm or separate the functions associated with the provision of service.

Removal of restrictions on access to the network became a generic feature of the Energy Policy Act of 1992, which gave FERC the authority to mandate wholesale transmission access. The objective was to promote a competitive bulk power market, and this in turn has led to considerable pressure for retail wheeling that would give retail customers the option of selecting from among rival suppliers of electricity. The California Commission was the first regulatory agency to issue a notice of proposed rule making (NOPR) in support of retail wheeling (1994).[7]

Serious questions can be raised as to whether this simplistic approach to open access is sufficient to promote a genuinely competitive market among buyers and sellers. There are a number of potential pitfalls. Interconnection between networks would still be voluntary; the formation of regional transmission groups could result in private regulation by agreement; private network planning could exclude many types of users; and it is far from clear that proceeding on a case-by-case basis to determine if sellers have market power is an adequate approach. Furthermore, there remains a question as to whether price caps for residual services provide adequate protection for core market customers. The price cap concept suffers from serious flaws as a device for controlling discrimination and cross-subsidization and assuring that captive customers participate in the joint production economies inherent in networks. FERC issued a massive NOPR on March 29, 1995, to pro-

---

7. See California Public Utility Commission, *Order Instituting Rule-making and Order Instituting Investigation of the Commission's Proposed Policies Governing Restructuring California's Electric Services Industry and Reforming Regulation*, R.94-04-031, I.94-04-032, April 20, 1994.

mote wholesale competition through open access.[8] But more analysis will be needed to determine whether emerging industry structures will support competitive markets and competitive prices, or whether bilateral oligopoly between major players will simply result in a redistribution of network economies on the basis of comparative bargaining power.

A second type of reform proposal focuses on industry restructuring that separates the network from those functions that will be largely deregulated. This approach was incorporated in the Rochester Telephone Plan that became effective on January 1, 1995. Structural separations have also been proposed by a number of electric utilities that seek to divorce the underlying transmission and distribution of power from the generation and marketing of power. Variants of the structural separations approach have been applied in the natural gas industry[9] and Canadian telecommunications,[10] and have been proposed by at least one regional Bell holding company.[11]

The Rochester Plan is the prototype for structural separations. Essentially, Rochester's telephone network remains under New York Commission regulation, while the marketing function for competitive services has been transferred to a largely unregulated affiliate. The network retains responsibility for providing basic service to everyone requesting it. The network will also provide unbundled access to all comers on the same terms as those provided to the unregulated affiliate. That is, it will supply comparable access to all rivals of the affiliate, including resellers, long-distance carriers, cable companies, and others. The network will have its own debt financing and a board of directors independent of the parent holding company. Since the network remains under regulation,

---

8. See Federal Energy Regulatory Commission, *Promoting Wholesale Competition through Open Access Nondiscriminatory Transmission Services by Public Utilities,* Docket No. RM 95-8-000, Notice of Proposed Rulemaking, March 21, 1995.

9. Structural separation in the natural gas industry was achieved when the pipelines abandoned the merchant function (i.e., purchasing gas on behalf of distribution companies) and confined themselves to transportation. The merchant function could be continued, however, through a separate marketing affiliate.

10. The Canadian Radio-Television and Telecommunications Commission adopted a novel approach to separation by "splitting the rate base" between utility and competitive segments, rather than turning to structural separation. See Telecom Decision CRTC 94–19, Ottawa, 16 September 1994, at 132.

11. For example, U.S. West announced plans to create two new classes of stock, one covering traditional phone assets, the other covering its cable and cellular phone business. Other Bell companies were reported to be considering similar steps. See Steven Lipin and Leslie Cauley, "U.S. West Plans Two Classes of Stock, Splitting Phone Holdings, New Ventures," *Wall Street Journal,* April 10, 1995, A-3.

the commission can fix rates for basic service and access, impose reporting requirements and quality of service standards (including penalties for poor performance), and, if necessary, restrict dividend payments to the parent if regulators suspect cross-subsidization or network denigration. The unregulated marketing affiliate is free to package and sell all types of competitive services (including basic service as a part of the package). It is also free to purchase capacity from the network or from any other source. The threat of bypass will serve to force the network to innovate and modernize. Finally, in the event that consumers wish to purchase telephone service from the local cable company, full number portability will be provided.

On balance, it would appear that this form of structural separation combines the best of both worlds—regulatory oversight of the network and entrepreneurial freedom to innovate in marketing and sales. Yet, there are questions that remain to be answered. For example, what are the boundaries of the network? Should it include landline as well as wireless services integrated into a total system? Also, should the network assume an active role in promoting new offerings or should it be essentially passive and wait for aggressive marketers to submit requirements?

Electric utilities have proposed structural separation plans to replace vertical integration. Under these plans the basic transmission and distribution network would remain under regulation, but generation would be spun off to a deregulated affiliate, as would power marketing at the retail level. Again, similar types of problems emerge. For example, how can the boundary be defined when generation and transmission may be substitutes? In such cases, they cannot be readily separated into discrete operating entities capable of dealing with each other at arm's length. Examples can also be drawn from natural gas supply, where storage and transmission could be substitutes.

What really emerges in electricity and gas is an apparent desire on the part of management to achieve greater profitability by exempting specific functions from direct regulatory oversight, and then transferring these properties to separate affiliates where they can be offered at market-based prices. In effect, the total network would be fragmented on the grounds that only transmission and distribution are natural monopolies. But British experience has shown that restructuring along these lines is vulnerable when duopoly or tight oligopoly exists in generation.[12] The same outcome could occur in the United States under the guise of retail competition.

---

12. See M. Smith, "Generators in Deal to Sell Plant and Reduce Prices," *Financial Times*, February 12, 1994, 1.

An alternative approach to structural separation in electricity would involve the creation of an independent, fully regulated, common-carrier grid. This grid would play a dominant role in expanding transmission, controlling generation through centralized dispatch regardless of ownership, and promoting integrated resource planning. Furthermore, the greater the size of the grid, the larger the number of potential buyers and sellers who would utilize it, with a parallel diminution of market power. But strong opposition to the grid approach can be expected from those who look toward the emergence of voluntary restructuring.

In summary, the search for reform must continue in the hope that some variant of structural separation, together with systemwide network pricing, will eventually emerge to promote network economies and distribute them in a fashion that maximizes societal welfare.

Market Failure in "Open" Telecommunication Networks: Defining the New "Natural Monopoly"

Lee L. Selwyn

PROPOSITION. *In any competitive market, individual firms will seek to acquire and to exercise monopoly power.*

COROLLARY I. *Those advocating "open" markets prior to their own entry are likely to change that position once their own incumbency in the market has been established.*

COROLLARY II. *Individual firms will continue to accumulate market power until the costs and risks associated therewith exceed the potential gains to be derived therefrom.*

Introduction

It is perhaps a truism of modern business that ownership of both Boardwalk *and* Park Place creates a far more valuable asset base than the sum of these properties' individual values. The game of *Monopoly* highlights one of several techniques for acquiring varying degrees of market power—controlling the entire supply. But there are other devices as well. *Product differentiation,* often accomplished through advertising campaigns, can produce limited market power by developing brand identification or by the creation of actual or perceived differences in features, quality, or other product attributes. The erection of *entry barriers* can be a particularly effective strategy for attaining *and for retaining* monopoly power in a market. Significantly for our present discussion, *network-based industries* are particularly vulnerable to the development of entry barriers through acquisition and control of multiple network elements.

In fact, the point at which Corollary II becomes operative will vary considerably from industry to industry; one might argue that the more a firm can successfully pursue the erection of barriers to entry by potential rivals before becoming subject to the constraints imposed by costs and risks, the closer that industry is to a "natural" monopoly. Where economies of scale and scope are present, the marginal gain (taken across the firm's entire asset base) from the acquisition of each additional asset will typically exceed the cost of that added component. This is particularly true in the case of networks of interconnected elements.

A Network as a Source of Market Power

In the past, efforts to identify and to quantify the presence of competition in telecommunication markets have tended to focus on the ability of individual suppliers or end users to acquire and to deploy transmission and switching facilities that are separate from those associated with public common carrier networks.[1] Often relying on purely anecdotal evidence, the presence of competition would be asserted if, for example, it could be shown that an individual user was capable of constructing his own private microwave or fiber-optic transmission facility or that a small, niche market provider had entered, was planning to enter, or perhaps was merely *permitted* legally to enter a particular market segment. The matter of interconnectivity among these isolated facilities was generally ignored, largely because of the failure to recognize the role of centralized control of network connectivity and the extreme economies of scale and scope that characterize large network structures. Most telecommunication network resources, particularly those associated with transmission, switching, and distribution, involve large fixed-capital investments that can be most efficiently recovered when the resource is shared among a large number of individual users or routes. Thus, the degree to which the owner of network resources is able to achieve an efficient scale and scope of operations will materially affect its ability to achieve and maintain an advantageous market position vis-à-vis present and future rivals. As we shall show, this property is intrinsic to large, complex networks and to the entities that control them.

Several examples are useful in illustrating this phenomenon. Figure 1 shows a simple two-point network interconnecting two locations, A and B. In fact, the *only* traffic that this simple network is capable of carrying is that generated by users at each of these two locations to one

---

1. Material in this section has been adapted from an earlier work by the author, "Assessing Market Power and Competition in the Telecommunications Industry: Toward an Empirical Foundation for Regulatory Reform," 40 FED. COMM. L.J. 193, 201 (1988).

Fig. 1. A two-point network

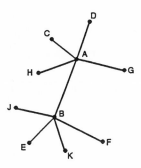

Fig. 2. A complex network

another; hence, the total cost of the facility must be recovered from these users. Figure 2 illustrates a more complex network in which the A-B link is interconnected to a number of other transmission links. In this case, in addition to carrying the A-to-B traffic, the same A-B link also carries traffic between C and B, D and B, A and E, C and F, and numerous other combinations. *As a general principle, the more segments in a communication network, the more traffic that will be handled by any individual segment,* all other things being equal. This property of networks engenders significant economic advantages to common carriers vis-à-vis individual users, and to large, ubiquitous common carriers vis-à-vis small, more specialized service providers.[2]

Networks and Market Power in the Airline Industry

This property of networks and its role in conferring market power on its owner can be readily demonstrated in the postderegulation airline

---

2. For example, local telephone companies can aggregate switched and dedicated services onto the same common network transport links, enabling them to achieve a far greater mass and level of utilization than a more specialized rival, such as a Competitive Access Provider (CAP) that only supplies circuit facilities for dedicated services.

industry, where the legal barriers to entry and competition have been largely eliminated and have ostensibly been replaced by competitive market forces.[3]

In the preregulation days, the Civil Aeronautics Board (CAB) had defined a "market" as generally consisting of a specific route between two (or a relatively few) cities.[4] Airlines would seek authority to enter and/or exit such "route" markets by making application to the CAB for each such route in question. Although airlines would each assemble collections of individual routes to form larger networks, the CAB's approach to regulation generally limited the actual economic benefits flowing from such networks to mainly operations and maintenance matters.[5] The agency, for example, regulated fares such that all airlines were required to charge the same fare for travel between the same pair of cities, irrespective of the routing (direct or connecting) or even whether a single or more than one airline participated in carrying the passenger from the point of origin to the ultimate destination. Indeed, the CAB *required* interline ticketing and joint fare construction such that passengers would realize no direct benefit from traveling on a single carrier nor suffer any penalty if they switched carriers in the middle of their trip.[6] Expressed in terms most familiar to those who deal with telecommunication issues, the CAB required that individual airlines allow passengers unrestricted *interconnection* among their respective route networks.

But airline deregulation has led to a fundamental redesign of those airline networks around "hubs" at which passengers may make connections to other flights, usually operated *by the same airline*. Under the "hub" system, the carrier fills its seats on each flight by combining local traffic (i.e., between the hub city and some other location) with through-traffic that transits the hub. Thus, flights into and out of the Northwest Airlines Detroit hub carry a certain amount of local traffic (where Detroit is either an originating or a terminating point for the trip), but predominantly carry traffic between points other than Detroit that transits the hub for purposes of making a connection. At the same time, there is no longer any requirement that joint fares be constructed at rates no higher than on-line fares, such that passengers entering the hub

---

3. Airline Deregulation Act of 1978, 49 USC § 1302(a)(9), (a)(10) (1982).

4. See Civil Aeronautics Act of 1938, § 401, 51 Stat. 977 (repealed 1958).

5. For a discussion of the economic effects of regulation in the airline industry, see George W. Douglas and James C. Miller III, *Economic Regulation of Domestic Air Transport: Theory and Policy* (Washington, D.C.: Brookings Institution, 1974).

6. For a discussion of fare construction, see William A. Jordan, *Airline Regulation in America* (Baltimore: Johns Hopkins University Press, 1970), 73–134.

via one carrier can be made to suffer a substantial fare penalty if they choose to switch carriers at the hub (if in fact that option is even available). In other words, carrier interconnection is no longer required by the CAB, and in fact it generally does not occur, other than at an administrative level.[7]

The consequence of this new network structure is that the presence of the network itself—coupled with the near-elimination of unrestricted interconnection—tends to confer market power and create substantial entry barriers that may be far more effective in limiting competition in these markets than the prederegulation route authority cases administered by the CAB. In fact, because of the enormous benefits that an airline may realize by filling more seats on existing flights, there are substantial economies of scale and scope that arise from the creation of the largest possible hub-oriented interconnecting network. To see why this is so, suppose that a flight segment between, say, Philadelphia and Detroit can support only 20 local passengers, but by providing connections at Detroit to Phoenix, Omaha, and Seattle, an additional 10 passengers destined from Philadelphia to each of these three cities will fly the same Philadelphia-Detroit segment, bringing the total passenger volume to 50. Now suppose the airline adds an additional destination to its Detroit hub (say Milwaukee) and that as a result another 10 Philadelphia-to-Milwaukee passengers will now take the Philadelphia-Detroit flight, bringing the total number of passengers to 60. Clearly, even in this highly simplified example, it is apparent that the more network points that are served by the central hub, the higher will be the occupancy level for each flight segment into and out of the hub. In fact, once an airline has established a major hub and has achieved a certain "critical mass" insofar as connecting-passenger volume is concerned, the presence of the hub and its associated route network creates an effective barrier to entry against other carriers who might seek to offer local two-point service (but whose passengers cannot interconnect with the hub carrier's network), unless that demand in the specific two-point market is sufficient *by itself* to fill up the airplane (e.g., New York-Washington, San Francisco-Los Angeles).

It has been suggested that this pattern of airline concentration is attributable to limitations on landing slots and gate space at the more

---

7. Interline airline ticketing is still supported administratively. However, as a general rule joint fares exist only where a carrier cannot provide end-to-end on-line connections through an intermediate transfer point. As hubs expand and trunk carriers enter strategic "code sharing" arrangements with regional commuter airlines, the incidence of such joint fare construction, at least with respect to domestic U.S. routes, is becoming quite rare.

congested airports. This physical constraint may, however, be a second-order effect of the network connectivity phenomenon. For example, airports with particularly severe landing and gate constraints—New York LaGuardia and Washington National—do not exhibit the same high levels of concentration as exists in less constrained markets, such as Minneapolis, St. Louis, and Pittsburgh. The entry barrier confronting the nondominant carriers at fortress hubs cannot be cured merely by allocating more gates or landing slots to these competitors; absent a highly interconnected network around the particular hub, the nondominant airline will simply be unable to fill up its airplanes.

Telecommunication Networks and Market Power
By viewing the airline industry in the context of *network relationships,* we can learn a great deal about the likely nature and extent of competition that can be expected to develop in the telecommunication field, particularly if some of the same corporate strategies and government policies are pursued. And what we learn is that the very property of networks that promotes consolidations and cartelization among airlines will also assure continued, indeed perpetual, market dominance by the incumbent telecommunication carriers within their respective market segments. The fundamental *networking* characteristics, not to mention scale and scope economies, that are evidently so important in the airline industry are, of course, enormously more important in the case of telecommunications, where interconnectivity and ubiquity work together to assure the dominant local and interexchange carriers virtually unchallengeable control of their markets. Indeed, even the nominal fungibility and sunk-cost conditions characteristic of the airline industry are even less conducive to competitive entry and exit in the case of common carrier telecommunications because, unlike airplanes, physical switching and transmission resources cannot be easily redeployed from a site of relatively low demand to one of high demand. Thus, the experience of "deregulation" and "competition" in the airline industry suggests that the pattern of networking and market dominance is likely to be significantly greater in the case of telecommunication carriers, because *(a)* they already have substantial ubiquitous networks in place, *(b)* these individual resources are characterized by far greater economies of scale than even the largest jumbo jets operated by the airline companies, *(c)* these resources are almost totally nonfungible and exhibit sunk costs of a magnitude comparable to their initial acquisition price, and *(d)* the confluence of these conditions creates an insurmountable barrier to entry within a given market segment.

A Network of Telecommunication Networks

This is not, however, to suggest that a single, ubiquitous network monopoly (not unlike the predivestiture, pre-MCI, pre-Carterphone AT&T) will ultimately reemerge, or that regulatory devices cannot be applied so as to promote competition where it is economically feasible. Indeed, experience over the past quarter century has demonstrated that there are limits to the beneficial accumulation of network assets, and that the various networks and network elements each present unique scale and scope economies.[8]

An "end-to-end" view of, for example, an airline transportation network would see it as embracing not only the intercity airline routes, but also the airports and local ground transportation facilities that bring passengers to and from those airports. While airlines might seek to monopolize intercity routes in and out of a given airport, they have not attempted even to enter, let alone dominate, the ground transportation business, and seem content to lease gate space from local airport authorities. Ground transport networks (such as the rapid transit line linking O'Hare with downtown Chicago) aggregate passengers for all airlines at a given airport, and dedication of these systems to a single intercity carrier would necessarily reduce their efficiency and perhaps make them impractical to build and operate. So, too, in telecommunication networks: postdivestiture experience has demonstrated that there are only limited scope efficiencies between local and intercity networks. Local exchange networks can and do efficiently aggregate traffic over common facilities for delivery to/from interexchange carrier networks; while the latter have certainly encouraged the development of competition in the provision of access services, they have generally not themselves elected to enter the local access market.

The initial focus of the 1974 antitrust case that ultimately resulted in the *Modification of Final Judgment* (MFJ) and breakup of AT&T[9] was on *vertical* integration of manufacturing with the provision of telecommunication services. Ironically, the divestiture itself was primarily aimed at

---

8. This revelation is hardly unique to the telecommunication industry. The corporate diversification and conglomeration craze of the 1970s and 1980s has largely been supplanted by "pure play" companies that can focus all of their management efforts and economic resources on a particular line of business. The recently announced plan by the Pacific Telesis Group to spin off its wireless subsidiaries highlights this 180-degree turn in U.S. corporate thinking.

9. *U.S. v. American Telephone and Telegraph Company,* 552 F. Supp. 131 (D. D.C., 1982), aff'd sub nom. *Maryland v. U.S.,* 460 U.S. 1007 (1983).

dismembering AT&T along *horizontal* lines, separating the provision of local services from long-distance services and the provision of customer premises equipment from local network access. As the postdivestiture configuration of network service providers began to take shape, it became apparent that the bifurcation of local and intercity networks would not (apart from the transaction costs incident to the transition itself[10]) impose serious inefficiencies or diseconomies of scale or scope. The key, of course, to this result was the fundamental requirement, imposed by the court and implemented by the FCC, that the divested Bell Operating Companies (BOCs) *interconnect* their networks with those of AT&T and any other competing interexchange carrier. Local exchange carriers constructed switched access networks interconnecting Class 5 end offices with multiple IXCs, capturing the LECs' own scale economies by aggregating the IXCs' traffic while supporting an efficient traffic collection and concentration function that no individual IXC (including AT&T itself) could readily duplicate. The IXCs, in turn, focused their attention on the development of high-capacity intercity route systems that were capable of transporting large volumes of traffic over highly concentrated network links at extremely low cost.

Moving beyond the LEC/IXC Partition

The MFJ's focus on the LEC/IXC interaction seems rather simple when considered in the context of today's far more complex industry environment. LEC networks are being called upon to support a wide array of new services, applications, and, most importantly, new providers. The complexion of the LEC monopoly, while still as pervasive and powerful as it was before the breakup, has evolved in response to new demands, as well as to new technologies. At a minimum, the scope of the LEC monopoly has narrowed considerably and, barring fruition of the LECs' *political* initiatives to retain and extend their horizontal control of adjacent markets,[11] there is far less reason now to imagine the reemergence

---

10. These included inter alia, the network upgrades and reconfigurations required to support "equal access" interconnection for multiple interexchange carriers and resellers, and most recently the creation of the "800 database" form of access that will largely eliminate AT&T's historic advantages in this market. These network modifications were not inexpensive; presumably the economic gains from the competition that they facilitate will more than offset their multibillion dollar cost.

11. Almost before the ink was dry on the divestiture decree, the BOCs began to seek rescission of the line of business restrictions to which they had previously agreed. Moreover, since then, the BOCs have, at the state level, pursued aggressive legislative programs that would substantially reduce the extent and effectiveness of economic regulation while affording them far greater freedom to engage in aggressive pricing and restric-

of a telecommunication monolith. Today, in fact, the national telecommunication infrastructure can be segmented into a number of distinct classes of networks, each possessing certain (but varying) degrees of scale economies, but among which scale and scope economies are limited or perhaps even nonexistent. The following is probably not an exhaustive list of the possible network segments, but serves to illustrate the type of balkanization that will not produce an erosion of either scale or scope economies and that might well foster significant gains within each individual segment and for the industry as a whole:

Intercity networks
"Local" interoffice switching, transport, and switched-access networks
Subscriber line ("local loop") distribution networks
"Local" dedicated high-capacity leased-line access networks
"Local" wireless access and intercommunication networks
Enhanced and value-added services networks

Transactional efficiencies aside, there is no fundamental source of or basis for economies of integration among any of these segments. We have already seen that intercity and local access/transport networks can be efficiently interconnected and that, in the intercity service market at least, a reasonable (if not overwhelming) level of market competition has been achieved. Similar bifurcations can be imagined for other currently integrated network elements. For example, LECs currently control both the interoffice switching, transport, and access network and the subscriber line distribution network within their respective service territories. Separation of these two LEC functions could well permit competition to develop (if only on a limited, niche market basis) in one or both of these segments. However, by maintaining common control over both and, more importantly, over the interconnections between them, the LEC can readily frustrate entry into either.

Even if full separation among the various network segments is accomplished (either by government fiat or by voluntary industry initiative), the actual extent to which effective competition can reasonably be expected to arise in any specific segment will depend heavily upon the degree to

---

tive service provisioning practices. These efforts are frequently framed in an assertion of extreme competitive pressures requiring "flexible" LEC responses. At the same time, the LECs have pursued regulatory agendas in which they would be permitted to commit large sums to extensive network upgrades with assurance of full recovery of their investments, thereby effectively insulating their shareholders from the risks normally attendant on such capital spending programs.

which that segment exhibits "natural monopoly" characteristics. And these are most likely to occur either in segments characterized by substantial scale economies (e.g., the local subscriber loop distribution system) or by extensive network connectivity (e.g., local switching, transport, and carrier access). The presence of high fixed costs and large-capacity facilities can create substantial entry barriers, since the incumbent, for whom such costs are largely sunk, can readily underprice a would-be rival for whom the cost of first acquiring capacity may be steep. Indeed, while there is substantial rivalry among the three major interexchange carriers (AT&T, MCI, and Sprint), AT&T still enjoys a dominant market share and entry by other full-line, nationally based IXCs has not occurred, although limited frictional competition at the retail level is still present.[12]

High concentration and market power can also arise in the face of severe resource constraints, even if scale economies and network coverage are not critical elements per se. The structure of the cellular industry, with a highly limited frequency spectrum allocated to only two providers in each market, has created enormous market power for the two incumbent carriers, not so much because of inherent scale efficiencies or network interconnectivity,[13] but because the carriers have succeeded in extracting large economic rents from their control of the scarce electromagnetic spectrum. If the FCC approaches the current generation of wireless Personal Communications Services (PCS) with the same misconception of basic economic theory that was evident in the formulation of its cellular policies, it is reasonable to expect precisely the same result for these services as well.[14]

The FCC's treatment of cellular markets underscores the importance of the *Proposition* with which we began this discussion (in any

---

12. However, "switchless resellers" or "aggregators" have largely supplanted earlier retail competitors who performed their own switching and interconnection of LEC access services with leased interexchange facilities. Aggregators principally perform an arbitrage function that, ultimately, is likely to lead to a restructuring of bulk and retail tariffs by the facilities-based IXCs. As such, retail competition of this type cannot be viewed as either permanent or of particular importance to the long-run development of the interexchange services market.

13. Indeed, the ludicrous fragmentation by the FCC of the U.S. cellular industry into more than 700 microscopic service areas has largely prevented such efficiencies and connectivity from arising.

14. The FCC has been actively investigating the implementation and regulation of personal communications services (PCS). In July 1992, the commission proposed initial spectrum allocations, licensing procedures, and several possible definitions of geographic market areas for separate "narrowband" (900 MHz) and "broadband" (2 GHz) PCS services. See Gen. Docket No. 90–314, ET Docket No. 92–100, *Notice of Proposed Rulemaking and Tentative Decision,* FCC 92–333, adopted July 16, 1992, released August 14, 1992.

competitive market, individual firms will seek to acquire *and to exercise* monopoly power) and, more to the point, the futility of ignoring it. In cellular, the FCC sought to *legislate* competition by applying economic theory gleaned from the first week of a basic course in microeconomic analysis (i.e., that the presence of more than a single firm makes a market competitive), while essentially skipping the remainder of the semester. Economists have long understood the importance of resource constraints in creating monopoly rents, even in putatively competitive industries with large numbers of incumbents,[15] and it is hardly surprising that (in the absence of price regulation of cellular services) the market values of cellular franchises have soared.[16]

The goal of the industry restructuring inherent in the AT&T divestiture was the eradication of corporate ties among industry segments that could function efficiently as independent players. The predivestiture integration had the effect of creating *artificial* entry barriers, not because competition could not exist in a particular market segment, but because entry could be frustrated by (the former) AT&T's control of adjacent markets. However, as the Sorcerer's Apprentice came to discover when he tried to chop up the enchanted broomstick, dismembering one powerful entity only served to create a collection of equally powerful ones. The divestiture, standing alone, would have accomplished nothing *had the Court and the FCC not required full "equal access" and seamless interconnection.* Unfortunately, while the divestiture solution adequately addressed the principal concern at that time—i.e., the BOC/IXC relationship—it failed to comprehensively resolve the "adjacent market" problem.

To be fair to the authors of the divestiture plan, the full dimensions

---

15. I always liked to cite the example of taxicab medallions when I taught microeconomics in an earlier life. Although these are frequently issued by the thousands (New York City has issued some 11,000 taxi medallions), they typically trade at prices well in excess of $100,000 each. Indeed, to the extent that increases in taxi fares translate into increases in the market value of taxi medallions, the principal beneficiaries of a fare hike are usually not the drivers (whom the increase was nominally intended to benefit), but are instead the owners of medallions who purchased them prior to their jump in market value.

16. Cellular franchises have recently traded in the range of $250 to $300 per "pop," a valuation metric convention adopted by the cellular industry representing the total U.S. Census population of the franchise area. These "per pop" prices translate into roughly $10,000 per existing cellular subscriber. On this basis, the "paper value" of all wireline and nonwireline cellular operating licenses issued by the FCC falls somewhere between $80 and $100 billion. Inasmuch as something under $10 billion has been invested by U.S. cellular carriers in actual system construction, the "economic rent" element, which may be thought of as the capitalized value of future monopoly profits, is clearly the overwhelming "cost" component of this service.

of the market conditions that prevail today were not apparent at that time. As such, the scope of the MFJ's equal access/interconnection prescription has turned out not to be sufficient by itself to accommodate the pluralistic fabric of networks and network interrelationships that has emerged over the past decade. While the economic and structural distinctions between local access networks and intercity networks were readily apparent to the authors of the MFJ, the divestiture decree left a large gray area between the two, making it nearly impossible to draw a bright line to establish the boundary point where one ends and the other begins, and thereby frustrating at least some of the restructuring goals.

The source of this difficulty is a new construct created by the divestiture process itself: the local access and transport area ("LATA"). LATAs were defined to delimit the geographic scope within which a divested Bell Operating Company could furnish network services. With limited exceptions, network connections that cross LATA boundaries must be provided by an interexchange carrier, even if the same BOC furnishes local service on both sides of the LATA boundary. The MFJ for all practical purposes *mandated* competition at the *inter*LATA level, prescribing the adoption of "equal access" and the system of "access charges" through which IXCs would deal with the BOCs and other local telephone companies. The FCC had by then already authorized interstate network services competition, and most states with more than a single LATA quickly followed suit, at least at the interLATA level. However, the status of competition at the *intra*LATA level is still far from settled.

The theory under which LATA boundaries were initially established was basically reasonable: LATAs were prescribed as a geographic area embracing no more than one standard metropolitan statistical area (SMSA), subtending only a single Class 4 toll tandem switching office and lying wholly within a single state. The idea was that the network below the Class 4 level was intrinsically local in character and not subject to high concentrations of "intertoll" traffic over a limited number of high-capacity intercity links. Instead, intraLATA networks were viewed as supporting highly diffuse traffic broadly distributed over the entire geographic scope of the LATA. The framers of the MFJ correctly recognized the differences in the economics of local versus intercity networks, and devised the LATA as a device for institutionalizing this distinction in the postdivestiture industry model. There were, however, several flaws in the manner by which LATAs were established, and consequently, in the postdivestiture policies with respect to LATA-level competition that have emerged.

First, the LATAs themselves violate the basic MFJ prescription more often than they conform to it. Of the 161 LATAs initially proposed by AT&T and the BOCs, more than half involved one or more "exceptions" to the SMSA, "state line," or "Class 4" standards. The bases for these exceptions varied, but in general the court was persuaded by arguments centering around the *integration* of a local network across what would nominally be required to exist as a boundary. Single-LATA treatment was afforded most multistate metropolitan areas even when split by a state line.[17] Also, areas served by multiple Class 4 toll tandem switches were frequently included within the same LATA if some other basis for integration of the network could be justified. There was considerable variation among the individual regional Bell companies with respect to the aggressiveness with which each pursued expansive LATAs. As a result of all of these factors, the usefulness of the "LATA" as *the* definitive bright line between monopoly and competition was seriously undermined.

Besides the historic anomalies that affected the LATAs' birth, there have been significant technological and market structure changes since the 1982 settlement that fundamentally redefine the scope of the basic local service monopoly and that create the same kinds of market integration concerns at the BOC level that the original breakup was supposed to resolve. Specifically, even though they are confined to services wholly within each LATA, the BOCs do confront competition at various levels that they can, through their integration, serve to frustrate. To be sure, some competition that has emerged at the LATA level is driven more by market distortions than by competitive efficiency, and it is reasonable for the BOCs to seek to correct such distortions.[18] At the same time, it is patently unreasonable for LECs to block or frustrate economically bene-

---

17. These included Chicago/northern Indiana, Kansas City, Missouri/Kansas, Philadelphia, the entire state of Delaware, Washington, D.C., and suburban Maryland and Virginia, among others. "Corridor exceptions" were allowed for portions of the New York Metro and Northern New Jersey LATAs and for portions of the Philadelphia and Camden, N. J. LATAs, permitting the BOCs in each case to jointly carry cross-LATA traffic. See *U.S. v. AT&T,* note 9; LATA Order, 569 F. Supp. 990 (1983).

18. For example, BOCs rarely offered monopoly network services under volume-based pricing plans in which quantity discounts or package prices would be provided to customers who could commit to a large quantity of service. Costs frequently are, however, highly sensitive to quantity of service provided to a given customer, and it is not surprising that competitors directed particular attention to such customers. Although it can be argued (and I would certainly agree) that the failure of the BOCs to establish cost-based rates was discriminatory against large users and undoubtedly encouraged competitive entry, it is not unreasonable for the BOCs to now seek to correct their rate structure. They should not, however, be permitted simply to shift revenues away from competitive services and onto monopoly services without a solid cost basis, nor should competitors automatically obtain the right to block any such repricing merely because it will make competition more difficult.

ficial competition in adjacent markets through their control of bottle-neck facilities.

Where intraLATA switched services (i.e., toll) competition has been authorized, LECs have strenuously resisted efforts by their competitors to secure the very same kind of equal access that formed a key cornerstone of the MFJ. Providers of high-capacity digital access services (so-called Competitive Access Providers) have encountered numerous roadblocks in their quest for the right to "colocate" facilities in LEC central offices. Providers of enhanced and on-line information services have been frustrated in their efforts to achieve a truly "open network architecture" offering sophisticated physical and logical interconnection arrangements and creating a platform for the development and introduction of an array of new services.

The Limits of Competition

From the foregoing discussion, we have seen that connectivity within a network both enhances its overall value and utilization, and creates an effective barrier to entry by would-be rivals. We have seen that the mere existence of multiple suppliers of network services, without connectivity among their individual networks, will not lead to effective competition. We have seen that interconnection among networks, whether competing or complementary, can enhance competition, utilization, and the general welfare. Finally, we have noted that the extent of potential competition *within any given industry segment* depends critically upon the economic characteristics of that segment, the structure of its costs, and the capacity and availability of its resources. That notwithstanding, there is very little *economic* basis for horizontal integration across the principal industry segments, and for this reason public policy should devote particular attention toward eliminating those practices and structures that permit incumbents with market power in one segment to effectively monopolize an adjacent market. The primary device for accomplishing this policy goal is equal and open network interconnection.

It is noteworthy that the regulatory attitudes toward and regulatory concern with interconnection have been decidedly different in the case of airlines vis-à-vis telecommunications, a fundamental policy distinction that may well explain much of the success of the procompetitive stance of the FCC and of many state telecommunication regulatory bodies and, correspondingly, the utter failure of the airline deregulation initiative.[19]

---

19. Although some industry apologists may claim that deregulation has been beneficial for U.S. airlines, the demise of nearly all postderegulation start-ups coupled with the precarious financial condition of most survivors would seem to belie such euphoria.

Where the FCC has long pursued policies leading to unrestricted resale, equal interconnection, and "open" network access, the creators of the current "deregulated" airline industry model went in precisely the opposite direction. Preregulation joint fare rules were disbanded, and resale is strictly prohibited. Indeed, the air carriers have used these restrictions to lock in customers[20] and thereby to create new entry barriers, often more formidable than the prior regulatory process of competing for specific route authorities.

Deregulation per se is not the solution; indeed, continued regulation of those telecommunication segments that continue to control essential facilities and thereby to wield market power is critical to the promotion of competition in those other segments in which the entry and survival of multiple providers is both economically feasible and desirable. Continued regulation of the local exchange monopolies so as to constrain their prices and to force appropriate interconnection policies will ensure healthy and efficient competition in the larger telecommunication marketplace. Deregulation (or euphemisms therefor) will have precisely the opposite result.

While the pace with which the FCC and state public utility commissions (PUCs) have implemented their various interconnection initiatives may fail to satisfy many nondominant providers, it is clear that the basic policy is sound and is conducive to the future network of networks. The airline experience has shown that deregulation is not consistent with network interconnection, and that without interconnection there can be no viable competitive marketplace. While the scope of the local exchange monopoly may have narrowed, continued local exchange company (LEC) control of essential bottleneck resources will not erode with time and should not be assumed away. It would be wrong to pursue a regulatory strategy that contemplates or that is predicated upon the development of competition in all industry segments; indeed, to do so is to guarantee less, not more, competition, overall.

---

20. Frequent-flier programs and advance-purchase round-trip tickets are examples of such devices.

Transformation in the Electric Utility Industry

Rodney Stevenson and Dennis Ray

The electric utility industry is poised for substantial transformation. The traditional pattern of power supply and regulatory oversight that has endured for decades is being called into question. Two seemingly incompatible policy directives are emerging at the federal and state levels. Federal policies are moving toward reducing regulatory oversight and placing greater reliance on market forces for directing the electric utility industry's growth and development. However, state regulatory policies have been putting greater reliance on integrated resource planning. The purpose of this essay is to examine the policy directions at the federal and state levels.

The Electric Power Industry

Electric power is big business. U.S. electric utilities have a combined generation capacity of more than 700,000 megawatts and an annual production level of over 2,500,000 gigawatthours. Electric utility revenues exceed $180 billion. With an average annual investment of between $30 and $40 billion annually, total investment in electric plant and equipment is now more than $550 billion, approximately half of which is in nuclear generation.

Electric service is provided by some 3,200 electric utilities comprised of about 200 investor-owned utilities, 2,000 municipally owned utilities, 1,000 cooperatives, and 10 federal or state government entities. The investor-owned utilities generate and distribute approximately 75 percent of the electric power sold to end users.

Increasingly, new sources of generation are coming from nonutilities.

This essay served as a basis for and draws on "Market Forces and Planning by Regulation: Conflicts and Complementarities," *Utilities Policy,* October 1993.

89

Since 1989, over 50 percent of the new generating capacity in the United States has been provided by organizations other than traditional utilities. These alternative providers supply over 45,000 megawatts of power and 233,000 gigawatthours of energy—or 8 percent of the total U.S. electricity production. In 1991, alternative providers added 5,200 megawatts of capacity and in 1992 they completed an additional 6,300 megawatts.

The electric utility industry is comprehensively regulated. At the federal level, the Federal Energy Regulatory Commission oversees investor-owned utility accounting practices and regulates transmission and wholesale power prices. State regulators control end use rates, new plant construction, and many other elements of electric utility activity. Federal and state regulatory policy making is not extensively coordinated.

Even though electricity is provided by local monopolies, electric utilities are not insulated from competition. Electric utilities face competition for the provision of energy services from other forms of energy (oil, natural gas, solar, and so on) and from efforts to increase energy use efficiency. Electric utilities are facing growing competition in the provision of electric power.

Competition for the provision of electric power includes competition in the generation of power, competition in the sale of power at wholesale, and competition in the delivery of power to end users. Independent power producers (IPPs), affiliated power producers (APPs), nonutility generators (NUGs), qualifying facilities (QFs), and exempt wholesale generators (EWGs) have emerged as alternative providers of electric power. These alternative suppliers are in competition with traditional utilities to the extent that they supplant generation that otherwise would have been provided by the utility. However, because the alternative suppliers do not have transmission line access, their competitive force is limited to being alternative wholesale providers to the local electric utility.

Electric utilities compete with each other in the sale of wholesale and retail power. Competition at wholesale involves sales from one electric utility company to another. The extent of the wholesale competitive potential depends upon the degree to which the various utilities have access to transmission services. Competition in the sale of retail power exists in attracting and retaining: (1) customers along the boundaries of utility service areas; (2) customers who have multiple location options (industrial customers); (3) customers who can engage in on-site generation (cogeneration); and (4) customers who can choose a different organizational arrangement for the provision of electric power through the establishment of a municipal utility.

Regulation by the Market: Federal Regulatory Policies

In recent years federal policy has shifted toward reliance on market forces to regulate industries. Transportation, telecommunication, natural gas supply, and banking have been substantially deregulated. Market forces are being utilized to address several other concerns, such as environmental problems. In the electric utility area, the direction of federal policy has been toward reduced regulatory oversight.[1]

There have been two lines of federal policy development. One line of development has facilitated competition. The application of antitrust laws to the electric industry, the actions of the Nuclear Regulatory Commission (NRC), and the provisions of the Public Utility Regulatory Policies Act of 1978 (PURPA) have augmented competitive forces in the electric industry. The other line of development has been to reduce regulatory oversight. Federal Energy Regulatory Commission (FERC) decisions reducing regulatory oversight have not necessarily strengthened competitive forces. While wholesale power competition among electric utilities has been a primary area of federal policy concern, competition in the generation of power is the focus of most of the recent policy initiatives.

Promoting Competition

In the 1970s, the U.S. Supreme Court ruled that the antitrust laws apply to the electric power industry even though the industry is comprehensively regulated.[2] The courts also ruled that federal regulatory agencies had to consider competitive impacts in their regulatory decisions. Had the courts ruled that the antitrust laws did not apply to a regulated electricity utility, most of the competitive potential that exists within the industry would have remained unrealized.

Various actions of the NRC have complemented the impact of the antitrust laws. During the era of nuclear power development, the NRC was required to assess the competitive impact of building and operating nuclear power plants. As a consequence, many small utilities obtained transmission access, coordination, and other concessions that furthered the development of competitive power markets.

PURPA opened the generation market to nontraditional power suppliers. It required that electric utilities purchase power offered by

---

1. An overview of various federal policy initiatives and forms of competition is contained in J. L. Plummer and S. Troppmann, eds., *Competition in Electricity: New Markets and New Structures* (Arlington, VA: Public Utilities Reports, Inc, 1990).

2. See *Otter Tail Power Company v. U.S.*, 410 U.S. 366 (1973), and *Gulf States Utilities Company v. FPC*, 411 U.S. 747 (1973).

qualifying facilities. The purchase price was to be based on the utility's avoided costs (that is, the costs that the utility would not incur because it was not providing the capacity and energy supplied by the QF). QFs could be made exempt from traditional regulatory policies and procedures that apply to wholesale power sales. The FERC has the responsibility for granting QF status. State commissions have the responsibility for determining avoided costs and establishing contract provisions and payment streams. PURPA was a critical piece of legislation that led to the growth of alternative power suppliers.[3]

Reducing Regulation

The FERC has played a major role in the movement toward regulation by market forces. In the 1980s and early 1990s, the FERC moved strongly to replace its historical cost of service standard for pricing with market-based rates. The FERC approved various bulk power experiments (in Florida, the Southwest, and the West) for utilities that wanted to operate transmission transactions with less direct price control.[4] The FERC allowed the utilities to substitute a negotiated rate standard in place of the traditional split-the-savings rules for short-term power sales.[5] The FERC approved transmission rates that allowed the utility to charge prices in excess of costs to capture a portion of the economic gain arising from electricity sales wheeled over the utility's transmission sys-

---

3. The emergence of alternative power providers was further enhanced by the adoption of state bidding programs for selecting suppliers of additional generation capacity. States such as California, Colorado, Connecticut, Maine, Massachusetts, and New York have used bidding programs. Under these programs, the utility is required to solicit bids for new capacity. The utility is generally required to specify its own avoided cost as the upper price level and to accept the best proposals. Generally, latitude is given in the decision process for other factors besides price (such as the experience of the bidder, likelihood of project completion, and dispatchability). Since 1987 several hundred bids have been made. The size of the generating facilities offered by the bidders have ranged from 1 to 1,300 megawatts.

4. For a description of the Florida Electric Power Coordinating Group, see "Butler Bulks at Extensive Utility Oversight: Discloses Brokering Project," *Inside FERC,* April 5, 1982. For a review of the southwest experiment, see J. Acton and S. Besen, "Assessing the Effects of Bulk Power Rate Regulation: Results from a Market Experiment," in Plummer and Troppmann, *Competition in Electricity.* The Western experiment (called the Western System Power Pool) is described in "Western System Power Pool Gets Go-Ahead," *Inside FERC,* March 16, 1987.

5. Traditionally utilities made short-term (for example, an hour ahead) power sales to each other on a split-the-savings basis, where the sale price would be halfway between the incremental operating costs of the two utilities. Starting in the mid-1980s, the FERC allowed utilities to negotiate a market price for short-term sales.

tem.[6] And for utilities that demonstrated an absence of market control over the buyer, the FERC allowed them to charge market-based prices for the sale of wholesale power.[7]

The "market-opening" pricing decisions made by the FERC were generally undertaken without first assuring that conditions necessary for a workably competitive market (such as nondiscriminatory transmission access) were in place.[8] When the FERC has employed "competitive tests" as a basis for deciding whether to allow a seller to set market-based prices, the tests have not been whether a workably competitive market exists, but a much weaker test based on the "limited market power of the seller" standard.

The Energy Policy Act of 1992 provided a basis for expanding deregulation and enhancing competition. The act expanded the number of generating entities that can be exempted from traditional regulatory controls such as standards for pricing and operation. Portions of the Public Utility Holding Company Act were deleted, making it easier for utilities to establish and expand "exempt wholesale generation" activity. The FERC was given clear authority to order transmission access (wheeling), but the extent to which the FERC will use this authority is still evolving.[9]

Vision and Status

The open market vision for the electric industry is that greater reliance on market forces achieved through increasing levels of deregulation will

---

6. The FERC's market-oriented transmission pricing policies can be seen in the following 1988–91 FERC Dockets: Turlock, ER88-219; Modesto, ER88–302; Public Service Company of Indiana, ER89-672; and Energy Services, Inc., ER91–569.

7. FERC Chairman Butler heralded the movement toward market-based pricing when he said in 1982 that ". . . the key to obtaining more active and efficient regional coordination markets may be looser price regulation . . . " as reported in *Inside FERC,* April 5, 1982. The FERC's movement toward a market-pricing policy for bulk power is seen in the following 1988–90 FERC Dockets: Ocean State Power I, ER88–478; Doswell, ER89–80; Commonwealth Atlantic I and II, ER90–24; Dartmouth Power ER90–278; and Cleveland Electric Illuminating, ER90–588. FERC has also supported market-based pricing by affiliates in the following 1989–91 FERC Dockets: Portland General Electric, ER89–581; TECO, ER90–164; Boston Edison, ER91–243; and Ocean State Power II, ER91–576.

8. While numerous hearings before the FERC focused on competitive issues, the agency has, by selective administrative deregulation decisions, done much more for the enhancement of the utilities' ability to price according to market forces than it has done for the emergence of competition.

9. For a discussion of recent FERC implementation activities, see David W. Penn, "Transmission Access, The Energy Policy Act of 1992, and FERC Implementation." Paper presented at the AMP-Ohio Annual Meeting, October 20, 1993.

stimulate the growth of a workably competitive industry. Increased competition will increase efficiency in the construction and operation of generating facilities, assure needed capacity additions to meet customer demands, reduce outage costs by development of greater supply diversity and utility flexibility in meeting customer needs, and reduce the costs of regulation. While the areas of competition are numerous, the degree of actual competition is subject to substantial debate.

Several questions about the vision and direction of the industry exist.

> Is it reasonable to expect that competitive forces will provide adequate and sufficient direction for assuring socially desirable outcomes in the electric industry?

> To the extent that competition is a desirable director in the electric industry, will the current pattern of increased reliance on market forces likely result in a more competitive environment?

> Should competition have desirable aspects for the ordering of the industry yet be insufficient to result in social optima, how might competition be combined with the various forms of regulatory oversight, such as integrated resource planning, to achieve the desired outcomes?

Regulation by Planning: State Regulatory Policies

Recently, state regulatory commissions have begun to use extensive planning mechanisms for regulating electric utilities.[10] Advanced planning mechanisms, first used in Wisconsin, New York, and California in the early 1970s, have been adopted in varying degrees by most states in the United States.

The new planning approaches are different from traditional utility planning processes. Traditionally, a utility proposes a specific project and the regulatory commission evaluates it. The utility forecasts de-

---

10. For a discussion of integrated resource planning, see M. Hanson, S. Kidwell, D. Ray, and R. Stevenson, "Electric Utility Least-Cost Planning, *Journal of the American Planning Association* 57, no. 1 (Winter 1991); F. Krause and J. Eto, *Least-Cost Utility Planning: A Handbook for Public Utility Commissions* (Berkeley: Lawrence Berkeley Laboratory, December 1988); C. W. Gellings, J. H. Chamberlin, and J. M. Clinton, *Moving Toward Integrated Resource Planning: Understanding the Theory and Practice of Least-Cost Planning and Demand-Side Management* (Palo Alto, CA: Electric Power Research Institute EM-5065, February 1987); and E. Hirst, *Regulatory Responsibility for Utility Integrated Resource Planning* (Oak Ridge, TN: Oak Ridge National Laboratory ORNL/CON-289, January 1988).

mand, screens supply-side options according to economic and financial objectives and engineering and environmental constraints, conducts detailed analyses of the selected supply-side option, and requests the necessary permits from governmental agencies. In response, the regulatory commission evaluates the utility's proposal relative to basic "threshold" concerns such as demand growth, system reliability, technical feasibility, and financial implications.

With the traditional planning process, the utility generally does not evaluate supply-side and demand-side options on a balanced basis. The utility's selection criteria reflect private rather than social interests. Project evaluation is based on utility-specific rather than statewide or regional planning considerations. Regulatory evaluation considers only the specific proposal of the utility rather than an integrated plan for meeting energy needs over time. Intervenors concerned about regional energy needs, environmental quality, or social issues find it difficult to become involved in the process and are excluded from the early stages of planning.

Under "integrated resource planning," the planning process itself is changed to increase the options evaluated, the objectives considered, and the parties involved. Integrated resource planning focuses on developing a complete set of demand-side and supply-side options for meeting energy service needs while the traditional planning approach is supply-side-dominant. In addition, the integrated resource planning process involves a broad set of planning objectives and invites the participation of a range of parties and interests. Under this planning process, factors that had been treated as constraints (such as reliability levels) become choice options.

Market Barriers, Market Forces, and Planning

Economists typically view the market as an efficient means of resource allocation. Integrated resource planning, however, involves public participation in economic choices through nonmarket channels. Planning can improve resource allocation if there are market barriers that impede the beneficial functioning of competitive forces. Some of the barriers to beneficial competition in the electric utility industry include technological factors encouraging natural monopolies, environmental and social externalities, nonnegligible transaction costs, and information asymmetries.

Electric utilities experience extensive economies of scale in transmission, and to a lesser degree in generation. Scale economies do not exist for the number of distribution areas served, although economies of density tend to favor a single distribution service provider in a given service area. The technological or natural monopoly barriers limit effective competition and the desirability of relying on market forces for ordering an industry. Transmission access and improved economies of small-scale units counter the effects of technological constraints on the production and supply of electricity. However, transmission scale economies limit the possibility of a competitive transmission market and economies of density continue to favor a single service area distribution provider.

When technological barriers exist, rate regulation is desirable to avoid monopoly exploitation of utility consumers. Because of the impact of new plant construction on the costs of utility operation, state commissions seeking to protect consumers from excessive prices for utility service need to evaluate the necessity of new plant additions. In evaluating construction requirements, a commission needs to assess a proposed project in the context of the overall future needs of utility customers and against a backdrop of alternative options for meeting those needs—in other words, to engage in integrated least-cost planning.

Environmental externalities exist with regards to all stages of utility operation. Environmental threats include production of greenhouse gases, emission of sulfur and nitrogen oxides, exposure to ionizing radiation, thermal pollution, electromagnetic fields, aesthetic effects, and so on. Because of the interconnected nature of electric utility systems, and because electricity follows the path of least resistance, reliability externalities arise when consumption by one customer increases the possibility of outages occurring for other customers.

Competition—or reliance on market forces—is not an effective means of dealing with externalities. The market choices open to those who wish to ameliorate externality consequences are limited. A customer of the polluting producer can withhold purchase, thereby inducing a reduced level of production. The customer can pay the producer to not engage in particular production methods. Finally, the customer can buy out the producer and exert direct control over the means of production. The viability of any of these options depends substantially on the nature of transaction costs. Organizing boycotts is not costless; developing markets for purchasing producer restraint is not easy; and customer buyouts of producers are expensive. Thus, even though participants in the market may be externally affected by the production choices of the producers, transaction costs may be sufficiently high to obviate a market-based solution.

Integrated resource planning provides a means for addressing the market failure arising from environmental externalities. An integral part of least-cost planning involves assessment of the alternative environmental consequences of the various supply-side and demand-side options.

The public participation aspect of least-cost planning provides a vehicle for the economic empowerment of individuals who would otherwise not be direct market participants. For example, agents of future generations or locationally distant customers (such as those downwind customers who experience the effects of acidic deposition) would have a forum for making the adverse consequences of particular technology choice and resource utilization options known to decision makers, who presumably are attentive to broader social impacts.

Transaction costs can bias market choices away from socially desirable resource options. Many demand-side programs require appliance modification, the purchase of new equipment, or the training of users. While these services can be provided through the open market, the transaction costs of service provision are not negligible. In order to overcome the transaction-cost barriers to efficient deployment of demand-side options, many have argued that utilities should either be direct providers of conservation services or act as an agent for customers. However, since electric power companies make money selling electricity, few utilities have sought the role of conservation provider or broker to support public policy objectives.[11] Integrated resource planning provides a useful process for the consideration of the consequences of alternative levels of involvement by the utility in the provision of conservation services.

Utilities generally have good information about present and future supply options; customers generally do not. Such an information asymmetry limits the ability of consumers to make socially optimal consumption and conservation decisions. Likewise, utilities with good supply-side information but poor demand-side information cannot be expected to make supply response decisions that will be either socially or privately optimal. Nonutility providers are also at an informational disadvantage. Integrated resource planning serves both to foster a better information base and to provide for better dissemination of information within the utility and to nonutility entities.

From a neoclassical economic perspective, the market barriers discussed above hinder efficient resource allocation. Such barriers limit reliance on markets and underscore the need for integrated resource planning. The limits of markets and role for integrated resource planning are also supported from an institutional economic perspective.

Institutional economists see the economy as a constantly changing

---

11. Demand-Side Management (DSM) programs can be justified on economic efficiency grounds. Hobbs presents a "most value" efficiency criterion for DSM programs. B. Hobbs, "The Most Value Test: Economic Evaluation of Electricity Demand-Side Management Considering Customer Value," *Energy Journal* 12 (1991): 67–91.

and evolving phenomenon. The major economic problem for institutionalists is how to structure the forms of social and economic interaction so as to accommodate change in a facile and socially beneficial manner. Though technological change occurs constantly, the adoption of new technologies does not go smoothly. As Veblen and Ayres note, technological advancements may be beneficial to society but may pose threats to the existing economic power structure. Ayres argues that dominant economic concerns act "ceremonially" to thwart the adoption of new technologies. Though such efforts fail in the long run, delays in the adoption of new technologies result in lost cost savings and increased costs of social disruption when adaptation finally takes place. Increased reliance on market forces without a truly workably competitive environment reinforces such ceremonial tendencies. Integrated resource planning can both promote and accommodate technological progress and provide a mechanism for societally beneficial risk management by sharing power inherent in the choice of technological paths.

Market Forces and Planning

For the electric utilities, market barriers and social objectives mitigate against reliance on market forces as the primary ordering force for the industry, and support application of integrated resource planning principles. Integrated resource planning can promote cooperation and information sharing, increase awareness of the consequences of utility choices on the different segments of society, provide for shared decision-making authority, and sustain planning efforts over time. Competition is not, in and of itself, a barrier to effective integrated resource planning, but various movements toward greater reliance on market forces may well thwart socially desirable planning efforts.

The ability of state regulatory agencies to pursue integrated resource planning requires the cooperation of the utilities. Utilities are more likely to cooperate if the state commission maintains effective control over utility prices and supply additions. However, because of the impact of federal policy initiatives, traditional utilities are likely to shift their generation activities and acquisitions to exempt wholesale generators (EWGs). Increased reliance on EWGs will provide utilities with greater opportunities for avoiding state planning efforts. The tenuous status of the Pike County doctrine is likely to limit the ability of state commissions to assess the prudency of utility acquisitions from EWGs.[12]

---

12. The thrust of the Pike County doctrine is that FERC approval of a wholesale transaction does not mean that a state regulatory commission must accept the transaction

Likewise, since EWGs are exempted from most regulatory oversight, a shift of capacity and energy acquisition to EWGs is likely to limit the ability of the state commissions to investigate and determine the overall desirability of alternative approaches to meeting future customer needs, including the promotion of socially desirable demand-side management (DSM).

If state commissions are to be able to sustain socially desirable planning efforts, various safeguards are required. These safeguards include the extension of state regulatory authority over new plant construction by EWGs and over the acquisition of capacity, energy, and DSM by utilities.

The ability of state commissions to sustain open planning would be enhanced if utilities were foreclosed from acquiring power or DSM services directly or indirectly from an unregulated corporate affiliate and foreclosed from providing power or DSM services through an unregulated corporate affiliate entirely. These policies do not imply that competition is not desirable or beneficial. Competitive choice of suppliers, within the overall structure of socially desirable integrated resource planning, can be an effective mechanism for ensuring efficiency and accountability in the supply of energy services. With appropriate safeguards such as those discussed above, fair and effective competition can evolve within the electric utility industry. Without such safeguards, the federal movement toward greater reliance on market forces will greatly enhance the ability of existing utilities to capture economic rents and limit the ability of society to direct development of the electric utility industry in socially and environmentally desirable directions.

---

as being reasonable. See, for example, *Pike County Light & Power Company v. Pennsylvania PUC,* 465 A.2d 735 (Pa. Commw. 1983), and *Kentucky West Virginia Gas Co. v. Pennsylvania PUC,* 837 F.2d 600, 92 PUR 4th 542 (3d Cir. 1988).

Part 3

Introduction to Part 3: Pricing in Network Systems

James L. Hamilton

As the essays in this volume make clear, networks offer great economies in providing services. Furthermore, where network technology has been changing rapidly, the costs of network services have fallen dramatically. These essays also show that realizing network economies involves a variety of tasks. The specific ways and places that economies occur in a network must be identified, because the costs of each segment and connection are crucial to designing networks to minimize the costs of providing network services. Investment must be made in the network infrastructure. Then, once a network is built, efficient use of the network requires that its economies be passed along to the users of network services; users must bear any external costs that they impose on the network, such as by increasing congestion.

Conveying the realized network economies and diseconomies to users is a problem of pricing. Network users make choices in terms of relative prices. As the authors of essays in this volume write about networks and their technologies and costs, invariably they raise questions about pricing network services. Efficiency requires that prices not lead users to choose higher real-cost methods over those with lower real costs. Hausman, for example, asks whether some private networks are built because of mispricing of some services or segments of the public network.

For most products and services, relative price structures emerge from the process of market competition, as suppliers struggle among themselves to attract customers. Where customers can choose among alternative suppliers, those customers who can be served at low cost will be courted by low bids. In this way, the relative price structure that emerges conveys to buyers the relative costs of supplying them. And if capacity is insufficient to supply all customers, higher prices will then allocate capacity and impose "congestion" costs on customers. Competitive investment in infrastructure will bring price structures into line with relative costs. Thus, the competitive market, at least in its idealized form, enforces a price structure that conveys to buyers the relative costs of serving them.

Government regulation of network industries is also a process for designing price structure. The regulatory process also could, at least in its idealized form, set prices that convey to users the relative costs that the regulated industry incurs in serving them and that allocate scarce capacity.

The problem of finding a proper mix of the competitive process and the regulatory process in designing price structures for network services appears in several essays in this volume. The deregulation movement of the past two decades has tried to push the mix more toward the competitive process and away from the regulatory process. The issue has been how to use the strengths of competitive markets. On the other side of the coin, the issue has been to find where the regulatory process is still superior to markets and competition. For air passenger fares and stock brokerage commissions, regulatory rate-setting processes have been entirely abandoned in favor of market competition. Telephone tariffs have been set in a process that mixes market competition in some segments of the network and regulation in other segments.

But even for industries where the regulatory framework is unavoidable, markets still might have some role in the price-setting process within the regulatory framework, and as a complement to the regulatory process. An example would be competitive generation and sale of electric power in wholesale markets, even if distribution must be regulated as a natural monopoly. Selwyn gives the example of a competitive auction of cellular frequencies within a regulatory structure.

In finding a balance between competitive processes and regulatory processes in pricing network services, a crucial matter is whether the sufficient conditions for competition are in place. Several authors who have written essays for this volume have raised this issue. If supplying the service is a natural monopoly, competitive processes must have a very restricted, supplemental role in setting prices. If suppliers are inherently few in number, the role of competitive processes will depend on whether the other forces for competition are sufficiently strong to counteract an oligopolistic market structure. Stevenson and Ray make the point that reducing regulatory oversight is not necessarily the same thing as creating a competitive business environment. Likewise, with specific reference to networks, an issue is whether interconnection among all rivals is essential for competition in networks.

One of these competitive forces is potential competition. If the threat of entry is sufficiently strong, then pricing may be approximately efficient notwithstanding the structural oligopoly. But the presence of structural oligopoly does raise all of the traditional questions about whether competition is sufficient to generate an optimal price structure and investment in infrastructure. These questions concern the height of barriers to entry and whether the oligopoly firms can devise strategies that deter entry. A crucial question is whether networks themselves may be a barrier to entry into certain service markets.

The essays by MacKie-Mason and Varian and by Borenstein are primarily concerned with market-pricing mechanisms and the sufficiency of competition in networks. Both depart, however, from the traditional public utility networks and discuss two other network industries. MacKie-Mason and Varian analyze the structure and operation of the Internet system of high-speed computer networks. Many persons now use the Internet without any thought about the structure and organization of that network. Borenstein is concerned with competitive entry into the air passenger transport networks as they have evolved into the new hub-and-spoke configuration. While MacKie-Mason and Varian and Borenstein move the discussion into different industries, the same issues about networks are still central, including the pricing issues.

MacKie-Mason and Varian propose ways that market mechanisms can have a role in governing use of the Internet. At present, incremental use of the Internet is not priced, which was not a problem until the Internet began to have periods of congestion. They propose a "smart" market mechanism that would impose rational pricing, in the usual sense of allocating congested capacity and signaling a need for investment to expand capacity. MacKie-Mason and Varian make the important point that using market mechanisms in networks has their own costs: transaction costs cannot be so high that they offset the efficiency gains from rational pricing. They propose that each Internet user attach a priority "bid" to each message, which would be used in congested periods to allocate scarce capacity to the highest bidders. Thus, MacKie-Mason and Varian present an excellent example of using competitive market mechanisms in networks.

Borenstein is concerned that the sufficient conditions for competition may be compromised in the air passenger transport industry by the air carriers' use of frequent-flier programs that reward customers for concentrating their purchases with one airline. Free tickets after some cumulative number of ticket purchases have greater value to customers as the tickets can be used for a greater number of possible destinations. Consequently, frequent-flier programs of the larger firms with larger networks of routes are more valuable to buyers, which gives those firms greater customer loyalty. When customers are attached to a particular air carrier in this way, Borenstein discusses conditions in which entry could be deterred and growth of competitors dampened.

Some Economics of the Internet

Jeffrey K. MacKie-Mason and Hal R. Varian

The High Performance Computing Act of 1991 established the National Research and Education Network (NREN). The NREN is sometimes thought of as the successor to the National Science Foundation Network (NSFNET), the so-called backbone of the Internet, and is hoped by some to serve as a model for a future National Public Network. Substantial public and private resources will be invested in the NREN and other high-performance networks during the next five to ten years. In this essay we outline the history of the Internet and describe some of the technological and economic issues relating to it. We conclude with a discussion of some pricing models for congestion control on the Internet.[1]

A Brief History of the Internet

In the late 1960s, the Advanced Research Projects Administration (ARPA), a branch of the U.S. Defense Department, developed the ARPAnet as a network linking universities and high-tech defense department contractors. Access to the ARPAnet was generally limited to computer scientists and other technical users.

In the mid-1980s the National Science Foundation (NSF) created six supercomputer centers that it wanted to make widely available to researchers. Initially, the NSF relied on the ARPAnet, Bitnet and several direct university links for this purpose, but planned from the beginning to

We wish to thank Guy Almes, Eric Aupperle, Paul Green, Mark Knopper, Ken Latta, Dave McQueeny, Jeff Ogden, Chris Parkin, and Scott Shenker for helpful discussions, advice, and data. Jeffrey K. MacKie-Mason was in residence at the Department of Economics, University of Oslo, when this paper was completed.

1. A glossary with many of the technical terms and acronyms we use can be found at the end of the essay.

develop a network connecting the centers. The planners of this new network, the NSFNET, designed it to provide connectivity for a wide variety of research and educational uses, not just for the supercomputers.[2]

The NSFNET was conceived as a backbone connecting a group of regional networks. A university was connected to its regional network, or possibly to a neighbor university that had a path to the regional network. The regional network hooked into a regional supercomputer. All of the supercomputers were connected by the high-speed NSFNET backbone, and thus the whole network was linked.

This design was quite successful—so successful that it soon became overloaded. In 1987 the NSF contracted with Merit, the Michigan regional network, to upgrade and manage the NSFNET. Merit, aided by MCI and IBM, significantly enhanced the capabilities of the network. Since 1985, the Internet has grown from about 200 networks to well over 11,000 and from 1,000 hosts to over 2,000,000. About 640,000 of these hosts are at educational sites, 520,000 are at commercial sites, and about 220,000 are at government/military sites in the United States, with most of the remaining 700,000 hosts located elsewhere in the world. NSFNET traffic has grown from 85 million packets in January 1988 to 37 billion packets in September 1993. This is a 435-fold increase in just over five-and-a-half years. The traffic on the network is currently increasing at a rate of 6 percent a month, or doubling once per year.[3]

The NSFNET was funded by public funds and targeted for scientific and educational uses. NSF's Acceptable Use Policy specifically excluded activities not in support of research or education, and extensive use for private or personal business. This policy raised a number of troublesome issues. For example, should access be made available to commercial entities that wanted to provide for-profit services to academic institutions?

In September of 1990, Merit, IBM, and MCI spun off a new not-for-profit corporation, Advanced Network & Services, Inc. (ANS). ANS received $10 million in initial funding from IBM and MCI. One of the main reasons for establishing ANS was to "provide an alternative network that would allow commercial information suppliers to reach the research and educational community without worrying about the usage restrictions of the NSFNET" (Mandelbaum and Mandelbaum 1992, 76).

---

2. See Lynch 1993 for a brief but detailed history of the Internet.

3. The compound growth rate in bytes transported has been 5.8 percent per month from March 1991 to September 1993, and 6.4 percent per month from September 1992 to September 1993. This probably underestimates growth in Internet usage because traffic on alternative backbone routes has probably been growing faster. Current traffic statistics are available from Merit Network, Inc. They can be accessed by computer by using ftp or Gopher to host nic.merit.edu.

In November 1992, the responsibility for managing NSFNET Network Operations was taken over by ANS. Merit, however, retains responsibility for providing NSFNET backbone services.

In 1991 ANS created a for-profit subsidiary, ANS CO+RE Systems, Inc., designed to handle commercial traffic on ANSnet. It seems apparent that the institutional structure is developing in a way that will provide wider access to private and commercial interests. According to the Program Plan for the NREN, the networks of Stages 2 and 3 were to be implemented and operated so that they would become commercialized and thus industry would be able to supplant the government in supplying these network services. Indeed, in December 1992 the NSF announced that it would stop directly funding a general-use Internet backbone, and that has recently occurred.

Internet Technology and Costs

The Internet is a network of networks that all use connectionless packet-switching communication technology. Even though much of the traffic moves across lines leased from telephone common carriers, the technology is quite different from the switched circuits used for voice telephony. With this technology, a telephone user dials a number and various switches establish a dedicated path between the caller and the called number. This circuit, with a fixed allocation of network resources, stays open and no other caller can use those resources until the call is terminated. A packet-switching network, by contrast, uses statistical multiplexing to maximize use of the communication lines.[4] Each circuit is simultaneously shared by numerous users, and no single open connection is maintained for a particular communication session: part of the data may go by one route while the rest may take a different route. Because of the differences in technology, pricing models appropriate for voice systems will be inappropriate for data networks.

Packet-switching technology has two major components: packetization and dynamic routing. A data stream from a computer is broken up into small chunks called "packets." The Internet Protocol (IP) specifies how to break up a data stream into packets and reassemble it and also provides the necessary information for various computers on the Internet (the routers) to move the packet to the next link on the way to its final destination.

Packetization allows for the efficient use of expensive communication

---

4. "Connection-oriented" packet-switching networks also exist: X.25 and frame relay are examples of such.

lines. Consider a typical interactive terminal session to a remote computer. Most of the time the user is thinking. The network is needed only when data are actually being sent. Holding a connection open would waste most of the capacity of the network link. Instead, keystrokes are accumulated until an <Enter, Transmit> key is pressed, at which time the entire buffer is put in a packet and sent across the network. The rest of the time the network links are free to be used for transporting packets from other users.

With dynamic routing, a packet's path across the network is determined anew for each packet transmitted. Because multiple paths exist between most pairs of network nodes, it is quite possible that different packets will take different paths through the network.[5]

The postal service is a good metaphor for the technology of the Internet (Krol 1992, 20–23). A sender puts a message into an envelope (packet), and that envelope is routed through a series of postal stations, each determining where to send the envelope on its next hop. No dedicated pipeline is opened end-to-end, and thus there is no guarantee that envelopes will arrive in the sequence they were sent or follow exactly the same route to get there.

The transmission control protocol (TCP) breaks a user's data stream into packets and then reassembles them at the other end. Thus, TCP creates a virtual connection, to make the stream of separate packets look like a single session to a user's application. To identify and reassemble packets in the correct order, TCP packets add their own header to the data. The header contains the source and destination ports, the sequence number of the packet, an acknowledgment flag, and so on. The header comprises 20 (or more) bytes of the packet.

Once a packet is built, TCP sends it to a router, a computer that is in charge of sending packets on to their next destination. At this point IP tacks on another header (20 or more bytes) containing source and destination addresses and other information needed for routing the packet. The router then calculates the best next link for the packet to traverse toward its destination, and sends it on. The best link may change minute-by-minute, as the network configuration changes.[6] Routes can

---

5. Dynamic routing contributes to the efficient use of the communication lines, because routing can be adjusted to balance load across the network. The other main justification for dynamic routing is network reliability, since it gives each packet alternative routes to their destination should some links fail. This was especially important to the military, which funded most of the early TCP/IP research to improve the ARPANET.

6. Routing is based on a dynamic knowledge of which links are up and a static "cost" assigned to each link. Currently routing does not take congestion into account. Routes can change when hosts are added or deleted from the network (including failures), which happens often with about 1 million hosts and over 11,000 subnetworks.

be recalculated immediately from the routing table if a route fails. The routing table in a switch is updated almost continuously.

The data in a packet may be up to 1,500 bytes or so. Recently, the average packet on NSFNET carried about 200 bytes of data (packet size has been steadily increasing). On top of these 200 bytes the TCP/IP headers add about 40; thus about 17 percent of the traffic carried on the Internet is simply header information.

Over the past five years, the speed of the NSFNET backbone has grown from 56 Kbps to 45 Mbps (T-3 service).[7] These lines can move data at a speed of 1,400 pages of text per second; a 20-volume encyclopedia can be sent across the net in half a minute. Many of the regional networks still provide T-1 service (1.5 Mbps), but these, too, are being upgraded.

The transmission speed of the Internet is remarkably high. We recently tested the transmission delay at various times of day and night for sending a packet to Norway. Each packet traversed 16 links, and thus the IP header had to be read and modified 16 times, and 16 different routers had to calculate the best next link for the transmission. Despite the many hops and substantial packetization and routing overhead, the longest delay on one representative weekday was only 0.333 seconds (at 1:10 P.M.); the shortest delay was 0.174 seconds at (5:13 P.M.).[8]

Current Backbone Network Costs

The postal service is a good metaphor for packet-switching technology, but a bad metaphor for the *cost structure* of Internet services. Most of the costs of providing an Internet backbone are more or less independent of the level of usage of the network; that is, most of the costs are fixed costs. If the network is not saturated, the incremental cost of sending additional packets is essentially zero.

The NSF currently spends about $11.5 million per year to operate the NSFNET and provides $7 million per year in grants to help operate the regional networks.[9] There is also an NSF grant program to help

---

7. In fact, although the communication lines can transport 45 Mbps, the current network routers can support only 22.5 Mbps service. Kbps is thousand (kilo) bits per second; Mbps is million (mega) bits per second. See the glossary in this essay for definitions of T-3 and T-1 service.

8. While preparing the final manuscript we repeated our delay experiment for 20 days in October–November, 1993. The range in delay times between Ann Arbor and Norway was then 0.153 seconds and 0.303 seconds.

9. The regional network providers generally set their charges to recover the remainder of their costs, but there is also some subsidization from state governments at the regional level.

colleges and universities to connect to the NSFNET. Using the conservative estimate of 1 million hosts and 10 million users, this implies that the NSF subsidy of the Internet is less than $20 per year per host, and less than $2 per year per user.

Total salaries and wages for NSFNET have increased by a little more than one-half (about 68 percent nominal) over 1988–91, during a time when the number of packets delivered has increased 128 times.[10] It is difficult to calculate total costs because of large in-kind contributions by IBM and MCI during the initial years of the NSFNET project, but it appears that total costs for the 128-fold increase in packets have increased by a factor of about 3.2.

Two components dominate the costs of providing a backbone network: communication lines and routers. Lease payments for lines and routers accounted for nearly 80 percent of the 1992 NSFNET costs. The only other significant cost is for the Network Operations Center (NOC), which accounts for roughly 7 percent of the total cost.[11] In our discussion we focus only on the costs of lines and routers.

We have estimated costs for the network backbone as of 1992–93.[12] A T-3 trunk line (45 Mbps) running 300 miles between two metropolitan central stations can be leased for about $32,000 per month. The cost to purchase a router capable of managing a T-3 line is approximately $100,000, including operating and service costs. Assuming 50-month amortization at a nominal 10 percent rate yields a rental cost of about $4,900 per month for the router.

The costs of both communication and switching have been dropping rapidly for over three decades. In the 1960s, digital computer switching was more expensive (on a per packet basis) than communication (Roberts 1974), but switching has become substantially cheaper since then.[13] We have estimated the 1992 costs for transporting 1 million bits of data through the NSFNET backbone and compare these to estimates for

---

10. Since packet size has been slowly increasing, the amount of data transported has increased even more.

11. An NOC monitors traffic flow at all nodes in the network and troubleshoots problems.

12. We estimated costs for the network backbone only, defined to be links between common carrier points of presence (POPs) and the routers that manage those links. We did not estimate the costs for the feeder lines to the mid-level or regional networks where the data packets usually enter and leave the backbone, nor for the terminal costs of setting up the packets or tearing them apart at the destination.

13. There is some mismatch between line and router capabilities. In the current design for a T-3 backbone, routers are relatively inexpensive compared to lines. However, in terms of performance, the switches are the bottleneck, and are likely to remain so for some time.

earlier years in table 1. As can be seen, in 1992 the line cost is more than thirteen times as large as the cost of routers.

The topology of the NSFNET backbone directly reflects the cost structure: lots of cheap routers are used to manage a limited number of expensive lines. We illustrate a portion of the network in figure 1. Each of the numbered squares is an RS6000 router; the numbers listed beside a router are links to regional networks. Notice that in general any packet coming onto the backbone has to move through two separate routers at the entry and exit node. For example, a message we send from the University of Michigan to a scientist at Bell Laboratories will traverse link 131 to Cleveland, where it passes through two routers (41 and 40). The packet goes to New York, where it again moves through two routers (32 and 33) before leaving the backbone on link 137 to the JVNCnet regional network that Bell Labs is attached to. Two T-3 communication links are navigated using four routers.

Technological and Cost Trends

The decline in both communication link and switching costs has been exponential at about 30 percent per year (see the semilog plot in fig. 2). But more interesting than the rapid decline in costs is the change from expensive routers to expensive transmission links. Indeed, it was the crossover around 1970 (fig. 2) that created a role for packet-switching networks. When lines were cheap relative to switches it made sense to have many lines feed into relatively few switches, and to open an end-to-end circuit for each connection. In that way, each

TABLE 1.   Communications and Router Costs (Nominal $ per million bits)

Year	Communications	Routers	Design Throughput
1960	1.00		2.4 kbps
1962		10.00	
1963	0.42		40.8 kbps
1964	0.34		50.0 kbps
1967	0.33		50.0 kbps
1970		0.168	
1971		0.102	
1974	0.11	0.026	56.0 kbps
1992	0.00094	0.00007	45 mbps

Sources: 1960–74 from Roberts 1974. 1992 calculated by the authors using data provided by Merit Network, Inc.

Note: Costs are based on sending one million bits of data approximately 1200 miles on a path that traverses five routers.

Partial NSFNET T3 Backbone Map

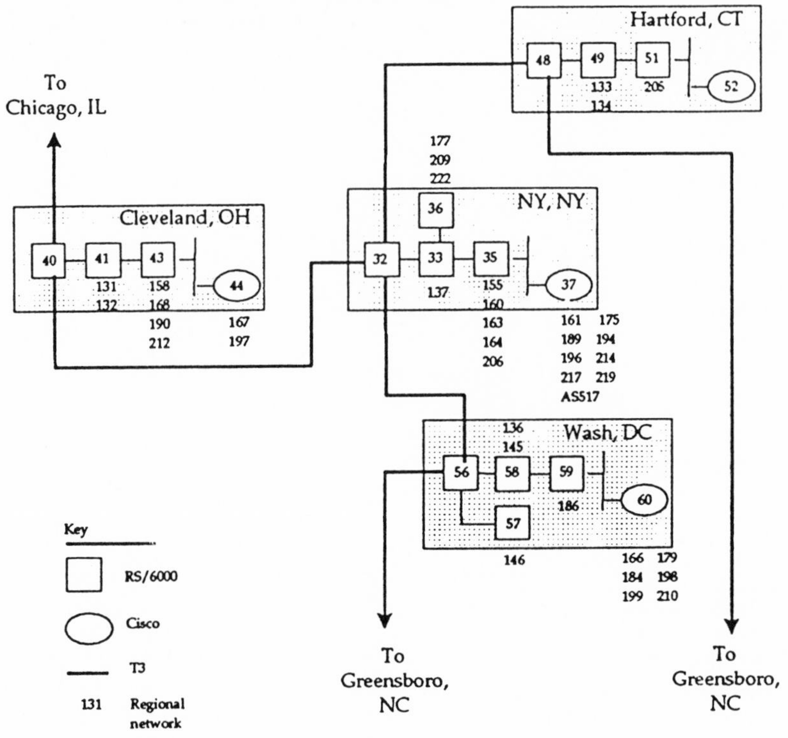

Fig. 1. Network topology fragment

connection wastes transmission capacity (lines are held open whether data is flowing or not) but economizes on switching (one setup per connection).

When switches became cheaper than lines, the network is more efficient if data streams are broken into small packets and sent out piecemeal, allowing the packets of many users to share a single line. Each packet must be examined at each switch along the way to determine its type and destination, but this uses the relatively cheap switch capacity. The gain is that when one source is quiet, packets from other sources use the same (relatively expensive) lines.

Although the same reversal in switch and line costs occurred for voice networks, circuit switching is still the norm for voice. Voice networks are not well-suited for packet switching because of variation in

Communications Line and Router Costs

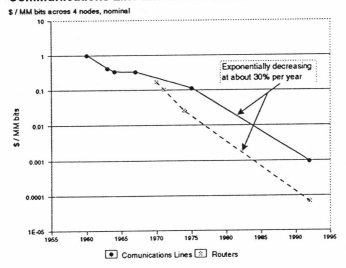

Fig. 2. Trends in costs for communication links and routers

delivery delays, packet loss, and packet ordering.[14] Voice customers will not tolerate these delays in transmission (although some packetized voice applications are beginning to emerge as transmission speed and reliability increase, see Stratacom, Inc. introduces "packetized voice system" 1986).[15]

Future Technologies

Packet switching is not the most efficient technology for all data communication. As we mentioned above, about 17 percent of the typical packet is overhead (the TCP and IP headers). Since the scarce resource is bandwidth, this overhead is costly. Further, every packet from a data

---

14. Our tests found packet delays ranging between 156 msec and 425 msec on a trans-Atlantic route (N = 2,487 traces, standard deviation = 24.6 msec). Delays were far more variable to a Nova Scotia site: the standard deviation was 340.5 msec when the mean delay was only 226.2 msec (N = 2,467); the maximum delay was 4,878 msec.

15. The reversal in link and switch costs *has* had a profound effect on voice networks. Indeed, Peter Huber has argued that this reversal made inevitable the breakup of ATT (Huber 1987). He describes the transformation of the network from one with long lines all going into a few central offices into a web of many switches with short lines interconnecting them so that each call can follow the best path to its destination.

stream must be individually routed through many nodes (12 seems to be typical for a transmission within the United States): each node must read the IP header on each packet, then do a routing calculation. Transferring a modest three-megabyte data file will require about 6,000 packets, each of which must be individually routed through a dozen or so switches.[16] Since a file transfer is a single burst of demand, there may be little gain from packetization to share the communication line; for some large file transfers (or perhaps real-time audio and video transmissions) it may be more efficient to use connection-oriented systems rather than switched packets.[17]

Packetization and connection-oriented transport merge in *asynchronous transfer mode* (ATM), which is gaining wide acceptance as the next major link-layer technology.[18] ATM does not eliminate TCP/IP packetization and thus does not reduce that source of overhead; indeed, ATM includes a 5-byte header in each 53-byte cell, imposing its own 10 percent overhead.[19] However, ATM opens end-to-end connections, economizing on routing computations and possibly reducing the overhead from network layer packet headers. Networks currently under development offer speeds of 155 and 622 Mbps (3.4 to 13.8 times faster than the current T-3 lines used by NSFNET). At those speeds ATM networks are expected to carry both voice and data simultaneously. A related alterna-

---

16. The average packet size is 350 bytes for file transfer protocol (FTP) file transfers, but for large files the packets will be about 500 bytes each. The header overhead for this transfer would be about 8 percent.

17. If there is a slower-speed link on the file transfer path—say 56 Kbps—then higher-speed links (T-1 or T-3) on the path will have idle capacity that could be utilized if the network was packetized rather than connection-oriented.

18. The link layer is another layer underneath TCP/IP that handles the transmission and physical congestion control for packets. Current examples of such technologies are Ethernet, FDDI, and Frame Relay. The link layer can carry "anyone's" packets; for example, TCP/IP packets, AppleTalk packets, or Novell Netware packets. Using the postal service analogy, the TCP/IP layer handles "get the mail from New York to Washington; the link layer specifies "mail from NY to DC should be packed in shipping containers and loaded onto a semitrailer bound for DC." In fact, ATM does not fit neatly into the standard open systems interconnection (OSI) seven-layer network model, because it embeds routing technology, which is traditionally the responsibility of the "network" layer, on top of the link layer.

19. ATM, in fact, adds even more overhead, depending on the ATM adaptation layer (AAL) protocol that is used to convert a stream of packets into cells and back again. AAL 3/4, originally designed to carry data packets such as TCP/IP, adds another four bytes of overhead per cell, for a total of 17 percent per cell, plus eight or more bytes per packet (there will typically be many cells per packet). A more efficient protocol, AAL 5, has been developed that adds almost no additional overhead per cell beyond the five-byte ATM header, although it still adds eight bytes per packet.

tive is Switched Multi-Megabit Data Service (SMDS) (Cavanaugh and Salo 1992).

ATM is promising, but we may need radically new technologies very soon. Current networks are meshes of fiber optics connected with electronic switches that must convert light into electronic signals and back again. We are nearing the physical limits on the throughput of electronic switches. All-optical networks may be the answer to this looming bottleneck.

The NSFNET backbone is already using fiber-optic lines. A single fiber strand can support one thousand Gbps (gigabits), or about 22,000 times as much traffic as the current T-3 data rate. To give some sense of the astonishing capacity of fiber optics, a single fiber thread could carry all of the network phone traffic in the United States, even during the peak hour of heaviest calling, on Mother's Day (Green 1991). Yet a typical fiber bundle has 25 to 50 threads (McGarty 1992), and the telephone companies have already laid some two million miles of fiber-optic bundles (each being used at no more than 1/22,000th of capacity) (Green 1991).

Thus, although switches are cheaper than lines at the rates that current technology can drive fiber communication, we should expect communication bandwidth to be much cheaper than switching before long. Indeed, it is already an electronic bottleneck that is holding us back from realizing the seemingly limitless capacity of fiber. When capacity is plentiful, networks will use vast amounts of cheap bandwidth to avoid using expensive switches.

"All-optical" networks may be the way to avoid electronic switches. In an all-optical network, data is broadcast rather than directed to a specific destination by switches, and the recipient tunes into the correct frequency to extract the intended signal. A fully functional all-optical network has been created by Paul Green and his colleagues at IBM. His Rainbow I network connects 32 computers at speeds of 300 megabits per second, or a total bandwidth of 9.6 gigabits—200 times as much as the T-3 based NSFNET backbone (Green 1992).

Despite their promise, all-optical networks will not eradicate the problem of congestion in the near future. Limitations on the number of available optical broadcast frequencies suggest that subnetworks will be limited to about 1,000 nodes, at least in the foreseeable future (Green 1991; Green 1992). Thus, for an internet of networks it will be necessary to pass traffic between optical subnetworks. The technologies for this are much further from realization and will likely create a congested bottleneck. Therefore, although the physical nature of congestion may change, we see a persistent long-term need for access pricing to allocate congested resources.

Summary

We draw a few general guidelines for pricing packet-switching backbones from our review of costs. The physical marginal cost of sending a packet, for a given line and router capacity, is essentially zero. Of course, if the network is congested, there is a social cost of sending a new packet, in that response time for other users will deteriorate.

The fixed costs of a backbone network (about $14 million per year for NSFNET at present) are dominated by the costs of links and routers, or roughly speaking, the cost of bandwidth (the diameter of the pipe). Rational pricing, then, should focus on the long-run incremental costs of bandwidth and the short-run social costs of congestion. More bandwidth is needed when the network gets congested (as indicated by unacceptable transmission delays). A desirable pricing structure is one that allocates congested bandwidth and sends appropriate signals to users and network operators about the need for expansion in capacity.

Congestion Problems

Another aspect of the cost of the Internet is congestion cost. Although congestion costs are not paid for by the *providers* of network services, they are paid for by the *users* of the service. Time spent by users waiting for a file transfer is a social cost, and should be recognized as such in any economic accounting.

The Internet experienced severe congestion problems in 1987. Even now congestion problems are relatively common in parts of the Internet (although not currently on the T-3 NSFNET backbone). According to Kahin: "problems arise when prolonged or simultaneous high-end users start degrading service for thousands of ordinary users. In fact, the growth of high-end use strains the inherent adaptability of the network as a common channel" (1992, 11). It is apparent that contemplated uses, such as real-time video and audio transmission, would lead to substantial increases in the demand for bandwidth and that congestion problems will only get worse in the future unless there is a substantial increase in bandwidth:

> If a single remote visualization process were to produce 100 Mbps bursts, it would take only a handful of users on the national network

to generate over 1 Gbps load. As the remote visualization services move from three dimensions to [animation] the single-user bursts will increase to several hundred Mbps. . . . Only for periods of tens of minutes to several hours over a 24-hour period are the high-end requirements seen on the network. With these applications, however, network load can jump from average to peak instantaneously. (Smarr and Catlett 1992, 167)

There are cases where this has happened. For example, during the weeks of November 9 and 16, 1992, some packet audio/visual broadcasts caused severe delay problems, especially at heavily used gateways to the Internet NSFNET, and in several midlevel networks.

To investigate the nature of congestion on the Internet we timed the delay in delivering packets to seven different sites around the world. We ran our test hourly for 37 days during February and March 1993. Deliveries can be delayed for a number of reasons other than congestion-induced bottlenecks. For example, if a router fails then packets must be resent by a different route. However, in a multiply connected network, the speed of rerouting and delivery of failed packets measures one aspect of congestion, or the scarcity of the network's delivery bandwidth.

Our results are summarized in figures 3 and 4; we present the results from only 4 of the 24 hourly probes. Figure 3 shows the median and maximum delivery delays by time of day. Average delays are not always proportional to distance: the delay from Michigan to New York University was generally longer than that to Berkeley, and delays from Michigan to Nova Scotia, Canada, were often longer than to Oslo, Norway.

There is substantial variability in Internet delays. For example, the maximum and median delays in figure 3 are quite different by time of day. There appears to be a large 4 P.M. peak problem on the East Coast for packets to New York and Nova Scotia, but much less of one for ATT Bell Labs (in New Jersey).[20] The time-of-day variation is also evident in figure 5, borrowed from Claffy, Polyzos, and Braun 1992.[21]

Figure 4 shows the standard deviation of delays by time of day for

---

20. The high maximum delay for the University of Washington at 4 P.M. is correct, but appears to be aberrant. The maximum delay was 627 msec; the next two highest delays (in a sample of over 2,400) were about 250 msec each. After dropping this extreme outlier, the University of Washington looks just like UC Berkeley.

21. Note that the Claffy et al. data were for the old, congested T-1 network. We reproduce their figure to illustrate the time-of-day variation in usage; the actual levels of link utilization are generally much lower in the current T-3 backbone.

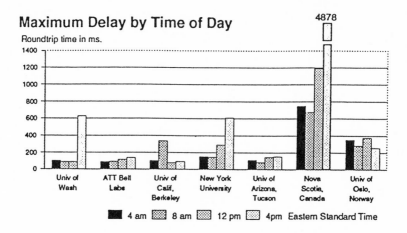

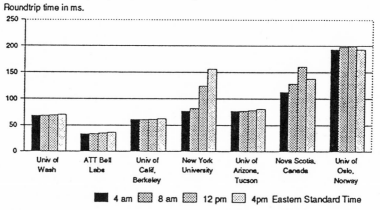

Fig. 3. Maximum and median transmission delays on the Internet

each destination. The delays to Canada are extraordinarily variable, yet the delays to Oslo have no more variability than does transmission to New Jersey (ATT). Variability in delays itself fluctuates widely across time of day, as we would expect in a system with bursty traffic, but follows no obvious pattern.

According to Kleinrock 1992, "One of the least understood aspects of today's networking technology is that of network control, which entails congestion control, routing control, and bandwidth access and allo-

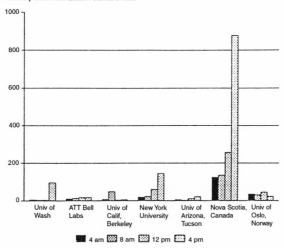

Standard Deviation of Delay by Time of Day

Roundtrip time in ms. Eastern Standard Time.

■ 4 am ▨ 8 am ▦ 12 pm ▨ 4 pm

Fig. 4. Variability in Internet transmission delays

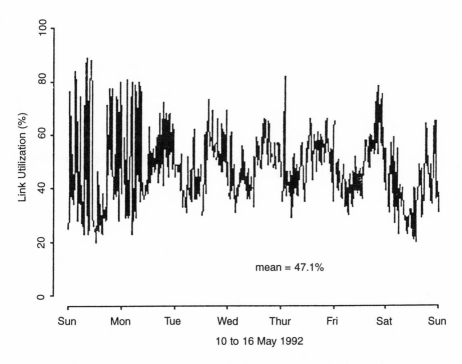

mean = 47.1%

10 to 16 May 1992

Fig. 5. Utilization of most heavily used link in each fifteen-minute interval. (From Claffy, Polyzos, and Braun 1992.)

cation." We expect that if access to Internet bandwidth continues to be provided at a zero cost there will inevitably be congestion. Essentially, this is the classic problem of the commons: unless the congestion externality is priced, there will inevitably be inefficient use of the common resource. As long as users face a zero price for access, they will continue to "overgraze." Hence, it makes sense to consider how networks such as the Internet should be priced.

As far as we can tell, this question has received little attention. Gerla and Kleinrock (1988) have considered some engineering aspects of congestion control. Faulhaber (1992) has considered some of the economic issues. He suggests that "transactions among *institutions* are most efficiently based on *capacity per unit time*. We would expect the ANS to charge mid-level networks or institutions a monthly or annual fee that varied with the size of the electronic pipe provided to them. If the cost of providing the pipe to an institution were higher than to a mid-level network . . . the fee would be higher."

Faulhaber's suggestion makes sense for a dedicated line—that is, a line connecting an institution to the Internet backbone—but it may not be appropriate for pricing backbone traffic itself. The reason is that the bandwidth on the backbone is inherently a shared resource—many packets "compete" for the same bandwidth. There is an overall constraint on capacity, but there is no such thing as individual capacity level on the backbone.[22]

Although we agree that it is appropriate to charge a flat fee for connection to the network, we also think that it is important to charge on a usage-sensitive basis, at least when the network is congested. After all, during times of congestion the scarce resource is bandwidth for additional packets.[23] The problem with this proposal is the overhead, or, in economics terms, the transactions cost. If one literally charged for each individual packet, it would be extremely costly to maintain adequate records. However, given the astronomical units involved there should be no difficulty in basing charges on a statistical *sample* of the

---

22. It may be true, however, that an institution's use of the backbone bandwidth is more-or-less proportional to the bandwidth of its connection to the backbone. That is, the size of an institution's dedicated line to the backbone may be a good signal of its intended usage of the common backbone.

23. As we have already pointed out, the major bottleneck in backbone capacity is not the bandwidth of the medium itself, but the switch technology. We use the term bandwidth to refer to the overall capacity of the network.

packets sent. Furthermore, accounting can be done in parallel to routing using much less expensive computers.

Conversely, when the network is not congested there is very small marginal cost for sending additional packets through the routers. It would therefore be appropriate to charge users a very small price for packets when the system is not congested.

There has been some recent work on designing mechanisms for usage accounting on the Internet. As a first attempt, ANS developed a usage sampling and reporting system it called COMBits. COMBits collects aggregate measures of packets and bytes, using a statistical sampling technique.[24] However, COMBits only collects data down to the network-to-network level of source and destination. Thus, the resulting data can only be used to charge at the level of the subnetwork; the local network administrator is responsible for splitting up the bill (Ruth and Mills 1992).[25] More recently, the Internet Accounting Working Group has published a draft architecture for Internet usage reporting (Internet Accounting: Usage Reporting Architecture, July 9, 1992 draft). Braun and Claffy 1993 describe measurement of Internet traffic patterns by type of application and by international data flows and discuss some of the accounting issues that need to be solved. We are also undertaking research on methods for reducing accounting costs.

Current Pricing Mechanisms

NSFNET, the primary backbone network of the Internet, has been paid for by the NSF, IBM, MCI, and the State of Michigan until the present.[26] However, most organizations do not connect directly to the NSFNET. A typical university will connect to its regional midlevel network; the midlevel network maintains a connection to the NSFNET. The midlevel networks (and a few alternative backbone networks) charge their customers for access.

There are dozens of companies that offer connections to the Internet. Most large organizations obtain direct connections, which are leased lines that permit unlimited usage subject to the bandwidth of the line. Some customers purchase "dial-up" service, which provides an

---

24. See Claffy, Braun, and Polyzos 1993 for a detailed study of sampling techniques for measuring network usage.

25. COMBits has been plagued by problems and resistance and currently is used by almost none of the midlevel networks.

26. NSF restricts the use of the backbone to traffic with a research or educational purpose, as defined in the Acceptable Use Policies.

TABLE 2.   Representative Prices for T-1 Connection

	Fee Components		
Service Provider	Annual Fee	Initial Connection Cost	Customer Premises Equipment
ALTERnet	24,000	8,900	incl.
ANS	32,000	incl.	incl.
CERFnet	20,100	3,750	incl.
CICnet	10,000	15,000	incl.
JvNCnet	33,165	13,850	incl.
Michnet	24,000	14,250	incl.
MIDnet	6,000	15,000	incl.
NEARnet	30,000	13,500	incl.
PREPnet	3,720	1,900	not incl.
SURAnet	25,000	3,500	3,300

Source: Compiled by Bill Yurcik, NASA/Goddard Space Flight Center, 11/13/92, with corrections by the authors.

Note: Prices as reported by the vendors. These are prices for a large university. There are some variations in the bundle of services provided, so the prices are not strictly comparable.

intermittent connection, usually at much lower speeds. We will discuss only direct connections below.

Table 2 summarizes the prices offered to large universities by ten of the major providers of T-1 access (1.5 Mbps).[27] There are three major components: an annual access fee, an initial connection fee, and in some cases a separate charge for the customer premises equipment (a router to serve as a gateway between the customer network and the Internet provider's network).[28] The current annual total cost per T-1 connection is about $30,000–35,000.

All of the providers use the same type of pricing: an annual fee for unlimited access, based on the bandwidth of the connection. This is the type of pricing recommended by Faulhaber 1992. However, these pricing schemes provide no incentives to flatten peak demands, nor any mechanism for allocating network bandwidth during periods of congestion. It would be relatively simple for a provider to monitor a customer's usage and bill by the packet or byte. Monitoring requires only that the outgoing packets be counted at a single point: the customer's gateway router.

However, pricing by the packet would not necessarily increase the

27. The fees for some providers are dramatically lower due to public subsidies.

28. Customers will generally also have to pay a monthly "local loop" charge to a telephone company for the line between the customer's site and the Internet provider's "point of presence" (POP), but this charge depends on mileage and will generally be set by the telephone company, not the Internet provider.

efficiency of network service provision, because the marginal cost of a packet is nearly zero. As we have shown, the important scarce resource is bandwidth, and thus efficient prices need to reflect the current state of the network. Neither a flat price per packet nor even time-of-day prices would come very close to efficient pricing.

Proposals for Pricing the Network

We think that it is worthwhile to think about how an efficient pricing mechanism might work. Obviously, our suggestions must be viewed as extremely tentative. However, we hope that an explicit proposal, such as we describe below, can at least serve as a starting point for further discussion.

We wholeheartedly adopt the viewpoint of Clark 1989, who says "It is useful to think of the interconnected [networks] as a marketplace, in which various services are offered and users select among these services to obtain packet transport." We take this point of view further and examine what kind of pricing policy makes sense in the context of a connectionless, packet-switched network.

There are many aspects of network usage that might be priced. Cocchi et al. 1992 make this point quite clearly and describe how a general network pricing problem can be formulated and analyzed. However, we will analyze only one particular aspect of the general network pricing problem in this paper: pricing access and usage of the network backbone.

The backbone has a finite capacity. If enough packets are being sent, some will be excluded or dropped. This decline in service quality imposes congestion costs on users. How should a pricing mechanism determine who can send packets at a given time?

General Observations on Pricing

Network engineers tend to take the behavior of the network users as fixed and try to adapt the technology to fit this behavior. Economists tend to take the technology as fixed and design a resource allocation mechanism that adapts the users' behavior to the technological limitations of the network. Obviously these approaches are complementary!

Let us consider some traditional pricing models for network access. One traditional model is zero-priced access. This is commonly used in highway traffic, for example. This has the well-known defect of the problem of the commons—if each user faces a zero price for access, the network resources tend to become congested.

Most common forms of pricing for network access use posted

prices: a fixed price schedule for different priorities of access at different times. For example, the post office charges a fixed price for different priorities of delivery service, and telephone companies provide a fixed charge for connections to different locations at different times of day.

The trouble with posted prices is that they are generally not sufficiently flexible to indicate the actual state of the network at a particular time. If, at a point in time, there is unused capacity, it would be efficient to sell access to the network at marginal cost, which is presumably close to zero. Conversely, if the network is at capacity, some users with high willingness to pay may be unable to access the network, even though other users with lower willingness to pay have access. Pricing by time of day helps to achieve an efficient pattern of usage of network capacity, but it is a rather blunt instrument to achieve a fully efficient allocation of network bandwidth.[29]

An Ideal But Impractical Solution

An "ideal" model for network access would be a continuous market in network availability. At each point there would be a price for access to the network. Users who were willing to pay the price for delivery of a packet would be given access; users who weren't would be denied access. The price would be set so as to achieve an optimal level of congestion.

How should the access price be determined? One mechanism would be a "Walrasian tatonnement." A tentative access price would be set. Users would examine the access price and see if they wanted access. If the sum of the demands for access exceeded the network capacity, the price would be adjusted upward, and so on.

The trouble with this scheme is that the user has to observe the current price in order to determine whether or not he wants access. If the time pattern of usage were completely predictable, there would be no problem. However, packet traffic on the Internet is known to be highly "bursty" and unpredictable.

A Smart Market

One way to alleviate this problem is to use a "smart-market" for setting the price of network access at different priorities.[30] In a smart market,

---

29. Posted, flat prices have some benefits. First, accounting and billing use resources too, and may be too high to justify. Second, many planning and budget officers want predictable prices so they can authorize fixed funding levels in advance.

30. The term *smart market* seems to be due to Vernon Smith. The version we describe here is a variation on the Vickrey auction.

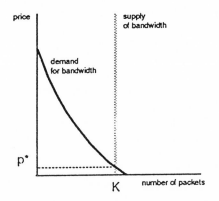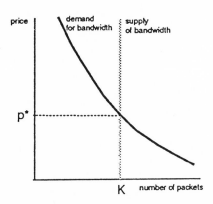

Fig. 6. Demand and supply for network bandwidth

users indicate only the *maximum* willingness to pay for network access. We will refer to this maximum willingness to pay as the user's "bid" for network access. The router notes the bid attached to each packet and admits all packets with bids greater than some cutoff value.

We depict the determination of the cutoff priority value in figure 6. The demand curve indicates how many packets there are at each different bid.

We take the capacity of the network to be fixed, and we indicate it by a vertical line in figure 6. In the case depicted, the demand curve intersects the supply curve at price p^*. Hence, this is the price charged to *all* users—even those who have packets with higher bids.

Note that the bid price can be interpreted as a priority price, since packets with higher bids automatically have higher priority, in the sense that they will be admitted before packets with lower bids. This is different from priority pricing by, say, the post office. In the post office model you pay for first-class mail even if there is enough excess capacity that second-class mail could move at the same speed. In the smart market described here, a user pays *at most* their bid.

The smart market has many desirable features. It is obvious from the diagram that the outcome is the classic supply-equals-demand level of service. The equilibrium price, at any point in time, is the bid of the marginal user. Each inframarginal user is charged this price, so each inframarginal user gets positive consumer surplus from his purchase.

The major difference from the textbook demand and supply story is that no iteration is needed to determine the market-clearing price—the market is cleared as soon as the users have submitted their bids for access.[31] This mechanism can also be viewed as a Vickrey auction where the n highest bidders gain access at the $n + 1$st highest price bid.[32]

We have assumed that the bid price set by the users accurately reflects the true willingness to pay. One might well ask whether users have the correct incentives to reveal this value: is there anything to be gained by trying to "fool" the smart market? It turns out that the answer is no. It can be shown that it is a dominant strategy in the Vickrey auction to bid your true value, so users have no incentive to misrepresent their bids for network access. By the nature of the auction, you are assured that you will never be charged more than this amount and normally you will be charged much less.

Remarks about the Smart Market Solution

Here we consider several aspects of using efficient prices for packet access to the Internet.

Who Sets the Bids?

We expect that the choice of bids will be done by three parties: the local administrator who controls access to the Internet, the user of the computer, and the computer software itself. An organization with limited resources, for example, might choose low bid prices for all sorts of access. This will mean that they may not have access during peak times, but still will have access during off-peak periods. Normally, the software program that uses the network will have default values for service— e-mail will be lower than telnet, telnet will be lower than audio, and so on. When special needs arise, the user can override these default values, for example to send an especially urgent e-mail message.

Note that this access control mechanism only guarantees relative priority, not absolute priority. A packet with a high bid is guaranteed access sooner than a low bid, but no absolute guarantees of delivery time can be made.[33] Rejected packets will be bounced back to the sender or buffered until congestion eases, or be routed to a slower network.

---

31. Of course, in real-time operation, one would presumably cumulate demand over some time interval. It is an interesting research issue to consider how often the market price should be adjusted. The bursty nature of Internet activity suggests a fairly short time interval. However, if users were charged for packets, it is possible that the bursts would be dampened.

32. Waldspurger et al. 1992 describe some (generally positive) experiences in using this kind of "second-bid" auction to allocate network resources. However, they do not examine network access itself, as we are proposing here.

33. It is hard to see how absolute guarantees *can* be made on a connectionless network. For a discussion of the types of guarantees that might be needed in future network design, see Shenker, Clark, and Zhang 1993.

Partial Congestion

In our discussion we have taken the network capacity to be exogenously given. However, it is easy to extend the mechanism to the case where an additional packet creates congestion for other packets, but does not entirely exclude them. To do this, we simply need to use an upward sloping marginal cost/supply curve, rather than a vertical one. We still solve for the same intersection of supply and demand.

Accounting

If the smart market system is used with the sampling system suggested earlier, the accounting overhead doesn't have to slow things down much since it can be done in parallel. All the router has to do is to compare the bid of a packet with the current value of the cutoff. The accounting information on every 1000th packet, say, is sent to a dedicated accounting machine that determines the equilibrium access price and records the usage for later billing.[34] Such sampling would require changes in current router technology, however. The NSFNET modified some routers to collect sampled usage data; the cost of the monitoring system is significant.

It is true that routers are the current technological bottleneck to faster throughput. As a result, some have criticized our smart market idea because it requires extra central processing unit (CPU) resources at the routers at the exact same time that the routers are a bottleneck. However, the routers are constrained in their ability to keep up with the speed of fiber-optic links, while switching and passing large data streams. Accounting and billing should impose much lower CPU requirements that can be handled in parallel by smaller, cheaper CPUs without appreciably slowing the congested routers. That is, accounting could be done on a separate machine that would not otherwise be able to reduce the routing bottleneck. Thus, our market may not substantially increase congestion at the router, while it *does* appreciably improve the prioritization of packet delivery during congested times.

Routing

The Internet is a connectionless network. Each router knows the final destination of a packet, and determines, from its routing tables, the best way to get from the current location to the next location. These routing tables are updated continuously to indicate the current topology (but not the congestion) of the network. Routing tables change to reflect failed links and new nodes, but they do not change to reflect congestion on various links of the network. Indeed, there is no standard measurement for congestion available on the current NSFNET T-3 network.

---

34. We don't discuss the mechanics of the billing system here. Obviously, there is a need for COD, third-party pricing, and other similar services.

Currently, there is no prioritization of packets: all packets follow the same route at a given time. However, if each packet carried a bid price, as we have suggested, this information could be used to facilitate routing through the Internet. For example, packets with higher bids could take faster routes, while packets with lower bids could be routed through slower links.

The routers could assign access prices to each link in the net, so that only packets that were "willing to pay" for access to that link would be given access. Obviously this description is very incomplete, but it seems likely that having packets bid for access will help to distribute packets through the network in a more efficient way.

Capacity Expansion

It is well known that optimal prices send the correct signals for capacity expansion, at least under constant or decreasing returns to scale. That is, if an optimally priced network generates sufficient revenue to pay the cost of new capacity, then it is appropriate to add that capacity. It appears from our examination of the cost structure of the Internet that constant returns to scale is not a bad approximation, at least for small changes in scale. Hence, the access prices we have described should serve as useful guides for capacity expansion. We have more fully described the role of congestion prices for guiding investment in MacKie-Mason and Varian 1995, which includes a simple analytic model of congestion pricing and capacity expansion.

Distributional Aspects

The issue of pricing the Internet is highly politicized. Since usage has been free for many years, there is a large constituency that is quite opposed to paying for it. One nice feature of smart market pricing is that low-priority access to the Internet (such as e-mail) would continue to have a very low cost. Indeed, with relatively minor public subsidies to cover the marginal *resource* costs, it would be possible to have efficient pricing with a price of close to zero most of the time, since the network is usually not congested.

If there are several competing carriers, the usual logic of competitive bidding suggests that the price for low-priority packets should approach marginal cost—which, as we have argued, is essentially zero. As a result, in the plan that we have outlined the high-priority users would end up paying most of the incremental costs of expanding the Internet.

In any case, our discussion has focused on obtaining an efficient allocation of scarce network resources conditional on the preexisting distribution of budgetary resources. Nothing about efficient pricing precludes the government from providing cash subsidies for some groups of users to allow them to purchase network access.

Role of Public and Private Sector

As we have seen, the Internet is growing at an astonishing rate. The economic setting is also rapidly changing. In December 1992, the NSF announced that it will stop providing direct operational funding for the ANS T-3 Internet backbone. The NSF intends to create a new very high speed network to connect the supercomputer centers, which would not be used for general purpose traffic. In addition, the NSF will provide funding to regional networks that they can use to pay for access to backbone networks like ANSnet, PSInet, Alternet, and SprintLINK. Meanwhile, the number of commercial vendors of Internet connections and services is rapidly growing, and most of the major telephone companies are getting into the market.

Recent mergers and joint ventures between phone companies, Internet providers, and cable TV operators make it clear that we are moving toward unified networks providing transport for data files, e-mail, voice, video, and other multimedia services. The economic issues of the Internet we have discussed are central to the development of markets for integrated services networks. In particular, current providers of access to the Internet generally charge for the "size of the pipe" connecting users to the network. However, the proliferation of services with widely differing requirements for bandwidth, bounded delay, packet ordering, and reliability will put enormous strains on backbones or network aggregators that allow unpriced usage of their links.

It is essential that efficient mechanisms for controlling congestion be developed. What has been missing in past efforts to design congestion control are mechanisms for decentralizing the setting of priorities for different demands on network resources. There must be a way to allocate congested bandwidth among millions of users with vastly different uses and different valuations for those uses. We think that usage-sensitive pricing is the most promising mechanism for accomplishing prioritization and socially efficient congestion control.

We have proposed a smart market idea for pricing congestion that has many attractive features. Our proposal is quite preliminary, of course. Several problems must be solved before it will be feasible to implement in a packet-switching network. Current TCP/IP protocols will not support a smart market, but the protocols are evolving. At the same time, technology is changing, so pricing and congestion-control mechanisms should be designed to be forward-looking and flexible. For example, the current momentum toward ATM suggests that traffic might be better priced at the ATM link layer rather than at the TCP/IP network layer in the future. ATM may provide a particularly good system in which to embed pricing because it offers connection-oriented service, and out-of-band signaling.[35]

The costs of using a smart market must be carefully weighed against the benefits. One point that we have tried to make clear, however, is that the costs of congestion are real, and are likely to increase dramatically. *Some* mechanism is needed; we hope our proposal stimulates constructive discussion of what mechanisms will be most effective.

There is an important role for the public sector in the evolution of a priced and commercialized Internet. It is very costly to redesign core protocols and implement them throughout the already massive base of installed hardware and software. Designing standards and protocols that can accommodate flexible pricing mechanisms must be done carefully, and work must begin soon. If governments want to see an efficient, competitive, and publically beneficial national information infrastructure, they should push now to develop a coherent model for pricing and economic congestion control. A privatized, integrated services Internet will not be viable without such standards.

GLOSSARY

Most of these definitions are taken from Malkin and Parker 1993.

Asynchronous Transfer Mode (ATM): A method for the dynamic allocation of bandwidth using a fixed-size packet (called a cell). ATM is one type of "fast packet."

backbone: The top level in a hierarchical network. Stub and transit networks that connect to the same backbone are guaranteed to be interconnected.

bandwidth: Technically, the difference, in Hertz (Hz), between the highest and lowest frequencies of a transmission channel. However, as typically used, it is the amount of data that can be sent through a given communication circuit.

Bitnet: An academic computer network that provides interactive elec-

---

35. Users generally want to know the price in advance for a connection, not for a packet, since a given session might send thousands or millions of packets, and prices can change dynamically in a congested network. Out-of-band signaling may help to solve some of the market administration details that are associated with our smart market and most other pricing mechanisms.

tronic mail and file transfer services, using a store-and-forward protocol, based on IBM Network Job Entry protocols. Bitnet-II encapsulates the Bitnet protocol within IP packets and depends on the Internet to route them.

circuit switching: A communication paradigm in which a dedicated communication path is established between two hosts, and on which all packets travel. The telephone system is an example of a circuit-switched network.

connectionless: The data communication method in which communication occurs between hosts with no previous setup. Packets between two hosts may take different routes, as each is independent of the other. IP and user datagram protocol (UDP) are connectionless protocols.

Gopher: A distributed information service that makes available hierarchical collections of information across the Internet. Gopher uses a simple protocol that allows a single Gopher client to access information from any accessible Gopher server, providing the user with a single "Gopher space" of information. Public domain versions of the client and server are available.

header: The portion of a packet, preceding the actual data, containing source and destination addresses, and error checking and other fields. A header is also the part of an electronic mail message that precedes the body of a message and contains, among other things, the message originator, date, and time.

hop: A term used in routing. A path to a destination on a network is a series of hops, through routers, away from the origin.

host: A computer that allows users to communicate with other host computers on a network. Individual users communicate by using application programs, such as electronic mail, Telnet, and FTP.

internet: While an internet is a network, the term "internet" is usually used to refer to a collection of networks interconnected with routers.

Internet (note the capital "I"): The Internet is the largest internet in the world. It is a three-level hierarchy composed of backbone networks (e.g., NSFNET, MILNET), midlevel networks, and sub networks. All Internet networks use the IP protocol, with multiple other protocols that run on top of IP.

Internet Protocol (IP): The Internet Protocol, defined in STD 5, RFC 791, is the network layer for the TCP/IP Protocol Suite. It is a connectionless, best-effort packet-switching protocol.

National Research and Education Network (NREN): The NREN is a U.S. government plan for an interconnected gigabit computer network devoted to high performance computing and communication.

packet: The unit of data sent across a network. *Packet* is a generic term used to describe a unit of data at all levels of the protocol stack, but it is most correctly used to describe application data units.

packet switching: A communication paradigm in which packets (messages) are individually routed between hosts, with no previously established communication path.

protocol: A formal description of message formats and the rules two computers must follow to exchange those messages. Protocols can describe low-level details of machine-to-machine interfaces (e.g., the order in which bits and bytes are sent across a wire) or high-level exchanges between allocation programs (e.g., the way in which two programs transfer a file across the Internet).

route: The path that network traffic takes from its source to its destination. Also, a possible path from a given host to another host or destination.

router: A device that forwards traffic between networks. The forwarding decision is based on network layer information and routing tables, often constructed by routing protocols.

Switched Multimegabit Data Service (SMDS): An emerging high-speed datagram-based public data network service developed by Bellcore and expected to be widely used by telephone companies as the basis for their data networks.

T-1: An AT&T term for a digital carrier facility used to transmit a DS-1 formatted digital signal at 1.544 megabits per second (Mbps).

T-3: A term for a digital carrier facility used to transmit a DS-3 formatted digital signal at 44.746 megabits per second (Mbps).

Transmission Control Protocol (TCP): An Internet standard transport layer protocol defined in STD 7, RFC 793. It is connection oriented and stream oriented, as opposed to UDP.

User Datagram Protocol (UDP): The user datagram protocol is a connectionless one-way mechanism for transmitting data.

REFERENCES

Braun, H.-W., and K. Claffy. 1993. Network analysis in support of internet policy requirements. Tech. rep., San Diego Supercomputer Center.

Cavanaugh, J. D., and T. J. Salo. 1992. Internetworking with atm wans. Tech. rep., Minnesota Supercomputer Center, Inc.

Claffy, K., H.-W. Braun, and G. Polyzos. 1993. Application of sampling methodologies to wide-area network traffic characterization. Tech. rep. Technical Report CS93–275, UCSD.

Claffy, K. C., G. C. Polyzos, and H.-W. Braun. 1992. Traffic characteristics of the t1 nsfnet backbone. Tech. rep. CS92–252, UCSD. Available via Merit gopher in Introducing the Internet directory.

Clark, D. 1989. Policy routing in internet protocols. Tech. rep. RFC1102, M.I.T. Laboratory for Computer Science.

Cocchi, R., D. Estrin, S. Shenker, and L. Zhang. 1992. Pricing in computer networks: Motivation, formulation, and example. Tech. rep., University of Southern California.

Faulhaber, G. R. 1992. Pricing Internet: The efficient subsidy. In B. Kahin, ed., *Building Information Infrastructure*. New York: McGraw-Hill Primis.

Gerla, M., and L. Kleinrock. 1988. Congestion control in interconnected lans. *IEEE Network* 2(1): 72–76.

Green, P.E. 1991. The future of fiber-optic computer networks. *IEEE Computer* 24, no. 9: 78–87.

Green, P.E. 1992. An all-optical computer network: Lessons learned. *IEEE Network* 6, no. 2.

Huber, P. W. 1987. *The Geodesic Network: 1987 Report on Competition in the Telephone Industry*. Washington, D.C.: U.S. Govt Printing Office.

Kahin, B. 1992. Overview: Understanding the NREN. In B. Kahin, ed., *Building Information Infrastructure*. New York: McGraw-Hill Primis.

Kleinrock, L. 1992. Technology issues in the design of NREN. In B. Kahin, ed., *Building Information Infrastructure*. New York: McGraw-Hill Primis.

Krol, E. 1992. *The Whole Internet*. Sebastopol, CA: O'Reilly & Associates.

Lynch, D. C. 1993. Historical evolution. In D. C. Lynch and M. T. Rose, eds., *Internet System Handbook*. Reading, MA: Addison Wesley.

McGarty, T. P. 1992. Alternative networking architectures: Pricing, policy, and competition. In B. Kahin, ed., *Building Information Infrastructure*. New York: McGraw-Hill Primis.

MacKie-Mason, J. K., and H. Varian. 1995. Pricing the internet. In B. Kahin and J. Keller, eds., *Public Access to the Internet*. Cambridge: MIT Press.

Malkin, G., and T. L. Parker. 1993. Internet users' glossary. User Glossary Working Group, User Service Area, Internet Engineering Task Force. Tech. rep., Xylogics, Inc. and University of Texas. Internet Request for Comments 1392.

Mandelbaum, R., and P. A. Mandelbaum. 1992. The strategic future of the mid-level networks. In B. Kahin, ed., *Building Information Infrastructure*. New York: McGraw-Hill Primis.

Roberts, L. G. 1974. Data by the packet. *IEEE Spectrum* 20: 46–51.

Ruth, G., and C. Mills. 1992. Usage-based cost recovery in internetworks. *Business Communications Review* 20: 38–42.

Shenker, S., D. D. Clark, and L. Zhang. 1993. A service model for an integrated services internet. Tech. rep., Xerox PARC and MIT. Internet Draft: draft-shenker-realtime-model-00.ps.

Smarr, L. L., and C. E. Catlett. 1992. Life after Internet: Making room for new applications. In B. Kahin, ed., *Building Information Infrastructure*. New York: McGraw-Hill Primis.

Stratacom, Inc. Introduces "packetized voice system" 1986. *Communications Week, 2.*
Waldspurger, C. A., T. Hogg, B. A. Huberman, J. O. Kephart, and W. S. Stornetta. 1992. Spawn: A distributed computational economy. *IEEE Transactions on Software Engineering* 18(2): 103–17.

Repeat-Buyer Programs in Network Industries

Severin Borenstein

While the cost advantages of network production are well recognized in many industries, and network demand complementarities have been studied as well, there has been less notice of the marketing advantages that multiproduct firms may gain in network industries. Repeat-buyer programs (RBPs), of which airline frequent-flier programs are best known, allow firms selling many related products to tie together consumption of those products in a way that may induce customer loyalty to the entire product line. Though frequent-flier programs are foremost in most consumer's recognition of these programs, the idea dates back to trading stamps issued before World War I, and in its simplest form probably has roots that run to the beginning of commerce.

Trading stamps enjoyed success in the first two decades of this century and again in the 1950s and 1960s, but have not become a permanent part of the retail scene.[1] Supermarkets, gas stations, and other retail stores have periodically launched RBPs that award one piece of a set of goods with each visit—cookware, dishes, glasses, and encyclopedias have all been given away piecemeal in order to induce return shopping visits. Music stores and, more recently, video rental outlets, have occasionally given away one free unit of the primary good they sell—records, compact disks, video rentals—after a certain number of previous purchases.

The modern use of RBPs in network or multiproduct industries is dominated by airline frequent-flier programs (FFPs), which are now

My thanks to Francine Lafontaine, Jeffrey MacKie-Mason, Wallace Mullin, and seminar participants at U.C. Davis and the Tenth Michigan Conference on Public Utility Economics for helpful discussions and comments. Jamie Woods provided excellent research assistance. Remaining errors are the sole responsibility of the author.

1. For the history and institutional description of trading stamps, I rely primarily on Fox 1968.

more than 12 years old and appear to be growing in popularity among consumers and airlines.[2] Many hotels and rental car companies have become affiliated with the airline FFPs, but those that have attempted to launch their own RBPs seem to have met with very limited success. Some credit card companies offer "discounted" purchases of selected goods after the card has been used for a certain amount of credit card purchases, also with apparently very limited consumer appeal. Long-distance telephone companies now employ similar marketing devices, giving away free or discounted telephone calls as well as other goods and travel services in return for repeat customer purchases, either by an individual subscriber or by a group of subscribers.

In the first section, I model repeat-buyer programs as marketing devices in the context of multiproduct firms that compete in one or many markets with similar firms. I demonstrate the conditions under which such strategies are most likely to be successful in protecting or expanding a firm's market share. I then analyze an array of RBPs that have been used in the United States over the last 30 years with varying degrees of success. The essay concludes with a discussion of the likely future prospects for RBPs.

A Model of Repeat-Buyer Programs

In their simplest form repeat-buyer programs (RBPs) are essentially just repeat purchase discounts: for example, buy 10, get the 11th free. RBPs differ from standard quantity discounts because they are based on *cumulative* purchases, not quantity purchased at one point in time, and because they are generally offered on goods that are not bought in bulk and stored.

An extremely simple model of RBPs points out one way in which such programs might deter entry by slowing the switch to a lower-priced entrant and, thus, by lowering the present value of the entrant's profits in the market.[3] Assume that each consumer buys at most one unit per period in a certain monopolized market and that the incumbent firm sells at the monopoly price of P_m. An entrant with lower costs could enter and immediately induce all customers to switch by charging a price just below the

---

2. After some reluctance, many European airlines have finally begun FFPs of their own and are studying how to expand them to be competitive with the U.S. carrier FFPs. See French 1991.

3. Klemperer 1987b has rigorously modeled the entry-deterring effects of consumer switching costs in general.

incumbent's unit cost.[4] Before the entrant appears, however, the incumbent could begin selling only in pairs (which are nontransferable or transferable only at significant transaction costs). A consumer would take delivery of one unit of the product in the period in which the pair is bought and one unit in the following period. The monopoly price of the pair would be $P_m + P_m/(1 + i)$, where i is the periodic interest rate. Consumption at that price and the present value of production costs would be unchanged from the case of unpaired sales. If entry occurs thereafter, about half of all customers will be in the middle of a pair of units and will not switch until at least one period after entry. The entrant's present value of profits after entry declines due to the incumbent's pairing of tickets, because the technique slows the rate at which customers switch to the entrant.[5] While this simple RBP may be effective in deterring entry, it is unlikely to afford one firm a competitive advantage against an existing rival in this simple setting.

Though this simple model highlights the effect of customer "attachment" with RBPs, it omits institutional details of the programs that seem to be important in their effectiveness. Many real RBPs exhibit increasing marginal payout functions over a wide range of cumulative purchases; for example, the extra RBP benefits from purchasing one more unit from a company increase as the total number of units purchased increases. Airline FFPs generally offer a bonus associated with 40,000 miles flown that is more than twice as valuable as the bonus available after 20,000 miles.

The extensiveness of the firm's product line also seems to be important in creating an attractive RBP. Hotels with facilities in many cities have used RBPs more extensively than those with a more limited number of outlets. Route network size seems to be important in the success of airline FFPs. FFPs have been cited as one reason that dominant airlines at certain airports are able to charge supracompetitive prices without inducing new entry.[6] The range of products offered, and their correlation in demand among customers, have two important effects. First, a larger range of products that appeal to a given customer means the customer is more likely to choose this firm over others if she intends

4. I assume Bertrand competition with constant marginal and average cost. The story is complicated only slightly by declining average costs.

5. Unlike the model presented by Banerjee and Summers 1987, this program does not discourage the incumbent from price cutting, because the firm offers a prepaid product for next period, rather than a discount off the market price of the good during the next period.

6. See Levine 1987; Borenstein 1989; U.S. Dept. of Transportation 1990; Borenstein 1991; and Borenstein 1992.

to concentrate purchases with just one company. Second, a larger range increases the set of bonus products that the firm can offer without purchasing them from other companies.

The type of bonus also varies substantially across RBPs in different industries. In the airline industry, the vast majority of bonuses are air-travel products, usually produced by the same airline. Long-distance telephone companies offer RBP participants long-distance telephone services as rewards, but also offer travel and some consumer goods. Hotel and rental car RBPs are as likely to give related travel products as the ones produced by the sponsoring company. At the other extreme, the trading-stamp RBPs made no connection between the product on which the stamps were earned and the bonus gift received. Similarly, credit card RBPs, such as Citibank's *CitiDollars* program, give discounts on unrelated products as the payoffs. Some credit card companies take this separation to an extreme by simply giving cash back to the holder of the credit card.

Finally, a distinctive feature of airline and certain other RBPs is that they can create a significant incentive conflict between the agent deciding which goods to purchase and the principal paying for the goods, a principal/agent problem. Airline FFPs offer a gift to the agent that does the buying for the business. Though such an incentive might raise a travel-purchasing firm's costs, RBPs can also increase the compensation received by its employees. Furthermore, such compensation is generally not taxed. Thus, one can easily imagine an allocation of costs and benefits from such schemes in which the only net loser is the Internal Revenue Service.[7] The potential for inefficient outcomes and anticompetitive effects from these RBPs remains, of course.

With these features of the programs in mind, I present a model of a simple RBP that may give a competitive advantage to a dominant firm and may deter entry. Though the model is quite stylized, it is likely that the insights from it are more general. I make the following assumptions:

- *a)* An incumbent monopolist serves two markets, A and B, each at constant average (equal marginal) cost, C_A and C_B, respectively.
- *b)* There are many consumers in market A, each of whom has a positive reservation price for 2 units per period on the market, R for the first unit and V for the second unit, where $R > V$ and

---

7. This may explain why firms that are large purchasers of air travel, such as Ford and General Motors, have not objected vehemently to frequent-flier programs. Few firms have implemented strict monitoring of frequent-flier miles acquired by their employees during business trips.

$C_A < V < (R + C_A)/2$.[8] One of the market A customers also purchases in market B. She receives positive value from one unit per period in market B, for which she has reservation price $R(>C_B)$. The other market A customers make no other purchases and no one else buys in market B.

c) At some point in time after the incumbent has established its operations in the industry, a potential entrant appears that could sell in market B at constant average cost, C_E, where $C_E < C_B$.

d) There are sunk costs associated with each market entered, S, which must be paid in the period before entry.[9]

Without an RBP, the incumbent charges $P = R$ in each market until the potential entrant appears. If the potential entrant decides to enter, it charges $P_E = C_B - \epsilon$, where ϵ is an arbitrarily small positive number, and sells one unit in market B each period. The new firm enters market B if and only if

$$S < \frac{C_B - C_E}{i}. \tag{1}$$

The RBP helps to deter entry by delaying or preempting customers from switching to the lower-price entrant. This, in turn, lowers the present value of the entrant's expected profits and thus, for some levels of sunk cost, will deter entry. This RBP may not be the optimal one from the point of view of the incumbent, but it is one example of an RBP that has this effect.[10] I assume that:

e) The RBP offered by the incumbent firm awards one free unit after every four that are purchased from the incumbent in either market. The bonus is awarded and consumed during the same period as the last purchased unit necessary to earn it. I assume that a bonus unit never "crowds out" an R-valued unit.[11] This

8. The restriction that $V < (R + C_A)/2$ implies that the incumbent would not find it more profitable to set $P = V$ than $P = R$. The importance of the fact that some positive-surplus purchases are left unsold without an RBP becomes evident in what follows.

9. The timing of the sunk-cost payment is completely arbitrary and has no effect on the conclusions.

10. See Caminal and Matutes 1990 for a model of equilibrium RBPs in a duopoly. Klemperer 1987a studies the effects of switching costs in general on rivalry among firms.

11. For people buying only in market A, this follows immediately from the restriction of same-period use of the bonus. It is an additional assumption for the customer who buys in both markets.

assumption is critical in the usefulness of RBPs. Its validity depends on the circumstances of the RBP as discussed in the following section. The assumption is consistent with the principal/
agent aspect of some of the programs.

f) Customers always choose to take their bonus units from market
A. Though this seems restrictive, it is not that unrealistic if one
thinks of market A as representing "all other" markets that the
incumbent serves.[12]

g) An immediate consequence of the RBP structure is that the
customer who consumes in both markets A and B earns the
bonus every second period.[13] A customer who has just received
the bonus is referred to as "unattached" and one who has some
units toward the next bonus as "attached."

h) Neither firm raises its price during a bonus cycle in response to
the number of units that a customer has built up toward her next
bonus. This is intended to be the one-customer analog to the fact
that there are always some RBP members who have investments
toward the next bonus. Alternatively, buyers could simply be-
lieve this to be the case, so that their valuations of future RBP
bonuses are made under the assumption that the firm will continue to charge its current prices.

Without entry, the incumbent firm charges a price higher than R in
market A, reflecting the reservation price for the first unit each period,
plus the market A customer's present value of the bonus unit, which is
valued at V when consumed.[14] Because the incumbent cannot separate
the customer who also consumes in market B from all other market A
customers, it is straightforward to show that the incumbent will not
change price in market A if entry occurs in market B. In the absence of
entry in market B, the incumbent charges a price above R in market B as
well, because the customer who earns the bonus every second period

---

12. Furthermore, a model with two paying customers in market B, one of whom
prefers the bonus in market A and one in market B, yields similar results.

13. The customers who consume only in market A earn the bonus every fourth
period.

14. To be precise,

$$P_A^* = R + \frac{V}{2 + i + (1 + i)^2 + (1 + i)^3}$$

This is the price at which the present value of payments over a four-period repeat-buyer
cycle equals the present value of the benefits of all units received during that cycle.

will receive a higher present value from it than those who receive it only every fourth period.[15]

Now consider the result of entry. With probability one-half, the customer has just received a bonus and is unattached. I consider this case first. If the customer chooses to switch to the entrant for her market B units, she will forgo the bonus that she would have received next period and every fourth period following that.[16] The present value of the forgone bonus units is

$$
\begin{aligned}
\text{Present Value of Lost} \atop \text{Bonuses from Switching} &= \frac{V}{1 + i} + \frac{V}{(1 + i)^5} + \frac{V}{(1 + i)^9} + \cdots \\
&= \frac{V}{1 + i} + \frac{V}{(1 + i)^5 - (1 + i)} \equiv V\Delta,
\end{aligned}
\tag{2}
$$

where Δ is a discounting factor defined by the last equality. Switching to the entrant, however, also lowers the incumbent's costs of providing bonus units. The present value of these cost savings is $C_A\Delta$.

Because of the cost savings from less frequent bonus awards if the customer switches, the incumbent will not be willing to lower P_B all the way to C_B to prevent switching. Instead it will drop only to $P_B = C_B + \frac{i}{1+i}C_A\Delta$, where the term $\frac{i}{1+i}$ converts the present value of the bonus to a perpetual charge, beginning this period. The incumbent would prefer to lose the customer than to lower price further in market B. Still, the entrant must offer the customer savings with a present value of at least $V\Delta$ in order to induce her to switch. That is, the entrant must undercut the incumbent's price by at least $\frac{i}{1+i}V\Delta$. Several results follow:

Result 1. If the market B customer is unattached and $C_E > C_B - (V - C_A)\frac{i}{1+i}\Delta$, the RBP prevents profitable entry regardless of sunk costs. If this condition holds, there is no price above C_E at which the entrant could make positive sales. In the subgame perfect Nash equilibrium, no

---

15. To be precise,

$$
P_B^* = R + \frac{V}{2 + i + 1/(1 + i) + 1/(1 + i)^2}
$$

The second term is the additional value of the bonus unit received by the person who obtains the bonus every second period rather than every fourth period.

16. That is, designating the time of entry as period 1, switching to the entrant will cause her to receive bonuses in periods 4,8,12, . . . instead of 2,4,6,8,10,12,. . . .

entry occurs. If entry were to occur, there is a unique Bertrand equilibrium in the subgame that follows in which the incumbent charges $P_B = C_E + V \frac{i}{1+i}\Delta - \epsilon$ and makes the only sale in the market.

Result 2. If the market B customer is unattached and $C_E < C_B - \frac{i}{1+i}(V - C_A)\Delta$, profitable entry will depend on the size of sunk costs, S, but will be less likely than if there were no RBP. If entry occurs, there is a unique Bertrand equilibrium in the subgame that follows in which the entrant charges $P_E = C_B - (V - C_A)\frac{i}{1+i}\Delta - \epsilon$ and makes the only sale in the market. So long as $V > C_A$, the entrant will have to charge a price discretely below C_B and thus the present value of future profits will be less than that without the RBP.[17]

Even if an RBP does not prevent an unattached customer from switching to a lower-price entrant, it could still dissuade switching by an attached customer until she becomes unattached. If, in a postentry equilibrium, an unattached customer would buy from the entrant, then her decision to switch while still attached instead of waiting one period would just delay all future bonuses. That is, instead of receiving bonuses in periods 1,5,9, . . . , where period one is the time of entry, a customer who switches while attached would receive bonuses in periods 2,6,10,. . . . This delay lowers the present value of future bonuses:

$$\begin{matrix} \text{Present Discounted Cost of} \\ \text{Switching while Attached} \end{matrix} = \frac{iV}{1+i} + \frac{iV}{(1+i)^5 - (1+i)} = iV\Delta. \quad (3)$$

Likewise, retaining an attached customer in market B for one period until she becomes unattached raises the incumbent's present discounted cost of providing bonus units by $iC_A\Delta$. These cost and value differences will be reflected entirely in the competition during the first period after entry, because all parties know that the customer will switch when unattached. Not surprisingly, it will be more costly for an entrant to induce an attached customer to switch than an unattached customer.

Result 3. If $C_B - i(V - C_A)\Delta < C_E < C_B - \frac{i}{1+i}(V - C_A)\Delta$, an unattached customer could be profitably induced to switch to the entrant, but an attached customer could not be profitably induced to switch until she became unattached. More generally, an attached customer will require a price $(1 - \frac{1}{1+i})i(V - C_A)\Delta$ lower than an unattached customer in order to induce switching.

Though quite simple in its structure, the model suggests a number of insights about RBPs.

---

17. The entrant will have to continue to charge P_E as long as the threat from the incumbent persists.

The RBP is effective because it allows the incumbent to tie, in a credibly precommitted way, the sale of a certain cumulation of items to a gift of another product that is valued more highly by the customer than it costs the incumbent to produce.[18]

Not only must the cost of producing (or acquiring) the bonus product be less than V for the RBP to be a profitable strategy, the *opportunity* cost of tying it as a RBP bonus must also be less than V. This is more likely to be the case if the V-value unit cannot be sold separately because of either an inability to price discriminate or the elimination of the principal/agent problem if it is sold directly. If the unit would otherwise not be sold, or would be sold by some other firm, whether in market A or some other "payoff" market (whose price would then determine an upper bound on V), then the RBP may facilitate a Pareto-improving trade.[19]

The value of the bonus unit V is compared to expenditures on the paid-for units in making the switching decision. If the shadow value of marginal expenditures on the R-value units is less than one, as is the case when the purchasing agent does not fully internalize price differences, then V is greater than the agent's actual reservation price for the unit and is thus a relatively strong inducement not to switch. The principal/agent aspect of an RBP reinforces its entry-deterring effect.

Because entry in market B would result in a price near marginal cost, $C_E < P_E < C_B$, the entrant would be at a disadvantage in establishing its own RBP. The only bonus it could offer, a free unit in market B, has an upper bound on its value of P_E.[20] Goods that normally sell for a price near marginal cost are poor candidates for bonus items.

---

18. Essentially, this is commodity bundling as explored by Adams and Yellen 1976. In contrast, if $V < C_A$, the RBP increases the cost to the incumbent of preventing switching more than it increases the customers' cost of switching.

19. If the incumbent can price discriminate perfectly, the RBP does not even deter entry if there are "attached" customers. With enough information for first-degree price discrimination, the incumbent could charge an attached customer exactly the gross surplus she derives from the units the firm provides. In that case, providing the unit in market B adds less to the consumer's gross surplus (the alternative being the entrant's unit at $P_E < C_B$) than it increases the incumbent's production costs. Instead, with entry, the incumbent's best response would be to sell the R-value and V-value units in market A for prices of R and V, respectively, and to let the entrant provide the unit in market B for $C_B - \epsilon$. If the RBP member wished to take the bonus unit in market B, the incumbent would buy that unit from the entrant rather than provide the unit itself.

20. This is true whether the entrant establishes new zero-point membership in its own RBP or offers to match the points that the customer has built up in the incumbent's RBP.

Versatility in the possible uses of a bonus raises the value of the bonus to a consumer by raising the option value. The incumbent that offers many different products of potential value to the consumer will be able to create a greater expected consumer-value-minus-cost differential with its bonus offer than an entrant that sells only a single product. The expansion of product line is important because it increases the consumer's expected value of the bonus unit, so the large product line should include many different choices that are likely to appeal to the type of consumer who is able to earn the bonus. Yet, at the same time, the bonus should be restricted so that it cannot be used for a unit that the consumer would otherwise purchase. A broad product line for bonuses can be created by purchasing bonus items from other companies, but these purchases are generally made at above marginal cost, so the net gain to the firm running the RBP will, in general, be smaller.

If the RBP does not deter entry, some of the customers in the entered market may choose to remain with the incumbent permanently, even though the incumbent always charges a higher price.

Welfare Effects of RBPs

The RBP modeled here has three direct effects. First, it enables the incumbent to bundle products to effect a Pareto-improving trade by selling the unit that otherwise would not be sold.[21] Second, it induces customer loyalty by raising the attached customers' cost of switching. Third, it sets up a principal/agent problem by paying bonuses to the purchasing agent in exchange for expenditures of the principal's money.

In the absence of competition or a threat of entry, the welfare effect of the RBP will depend on whether the surplus gain due to bundling outweighs the (possible) loss from the principal/agent problem.[22] If entry is possible, the RBP may "efficiently" deter it even though $C_B > C_E$, because sales on the B market also permit Pareto-improving exchanges of the bonus unit.[23] The RBP may also allow "inefficient" entry deterrence if switching fails to occur only because marginal expenditures by the principal are not fully internalized by the purchasing agent.

The loyalty induced from attached customers can be examined sepa-

---

21. This is a Pareto improvement so long as the purchaser's true reservation price for the bonus unit is above C_A.

22. The principal/agent problem will actually increase surplus if the agent's true reservation value of the bonus unit is greater than C_A. Still, the principal will lose if it doesn't receive the kickback itself.

23. This statement takes the structure and terms of the RBP as given.

rately from the other two effects. Consider an alternative RBP-like plan in which the incumbent gives a *transferable* coupon to every paying buyer of a unit, with four coupons being exchangeable for a bonus unit. Analysis of the bundling and principal/agent effects differs only slightly from the RBP model presented above.[24] With transferable coupons, however, the effect of attachment disappears. Switching to the entrant does not delay future bonuses, because no one holds an inventory of coupons.[25] In steady state, this RBP-like plan gives away the same number of units each period as the RBP modeled above. This plan, however, does not attach customers across periods and, thus, does not allow the credible commitment by the incumbent to maintain some proportion of the market after entry. Looking back at the very simple "pairing" model of RBPs presented at the beginning of this section, transferability of the second unit in the pair would destroy the advantage gained from such a RBP, as both units in a pair would be consumed in the period of purchase and no commitment by the incumbent for the following period would be credible. From these examples, it is clear that the attachment of consumers through an RBP is not critical to their use in affecting potential welfare improvements, but it is central to the role of an RBP as an entry deterrent.

In the full RBP model presented, the multiproduct incumbent has an advantage in part because V is likely to be higher for the bonus the incumbent offers. This raises the welfare improvement from tying and increases the entry-deterring effect of attachment (note the necessary price differential in result 3). It is worth noting that both of these effects disappear with an RBP-like transferable coupon system. The resulting market in coupons will channel each firm's coupons to the markets where users obtain the highest value from them. Firms with more extensive product lines, overall will still have some advantage, but there will be less value from offering a product line that appeals to a certain type of consumer. To apply this to the airline industry, even with the transferable coupon, the airlines with the largest systems will still have some advantage in using RBPs, but an airline with most of the service in a customer's city will have no particular advantage due to that local dominance.

---

24. A coupon system makes monitoring and recapturing kickbacks easier for the principal and makes it more difficult for the airline to prevent use of the bonus for R-value units, where each coupon has a market value of $V/4$ and each will be used in the same period issued. The entrant would have to undercut the incumbent's price by $V/4$ and would be able to do so only if $C_E < C_B - (V - C_A)/4$.

25. If a person does not intend to use a coupon in the period of acquisition, it is more valuable to sell it in the competitive coupon market and buy coupons back at the time a bonus unit is desired.

Repeat-Buyer Programs in Practice

Repeat-buyer programs have been used in many different industries and markets, with various degrees of success. I begin the application of the model in this section by discussing the least sophisticated programs: buy $n - 1$ and get the nth unit free. I then examine programs of increasing complexity, including trading stamps, airline frequent-flier programs, and RBPs currently in use in the long-distance telephone industry.

The nth Unit is Free

The least complex or sophisticated RBPs offer a free unit after a certain number are purchased. These plans, which are common in music and video markets, seem unlikely to have persistent benefits to the firms that use them. Clearly, they do not benefit from principal/agent separation in most cases. In quite a few instances, it seems likely that the bonus unit crowds out purchase of an additional unit, thus raising the firm's opportunity cost to the full retail price. Multiproduct or network considerations are weak in these cases, since most people rent videos and purchase music in a single town or neighborhood. In fact, these simple RBPs seem to be more common among small single-outlet retailers than in multi-outlet chains.[26]

Furthermore, these simple RBPs occur most frequently in markets with numerous competitors—most towns have many music and video stores—so that deterring entry is less valuable than gaining a competitive advantage over other incumbents.[27] As the model shows, an RBP can provide a competitive advantage to one firm over competitors without RBPs if it permits sale of some units that would otherwise go unsold by that firm due to its inability to price discriminate or take advantage of principal/agent separation. The infrequency of principal/agent problems in these markets along with the ease with which bonus units can replace a regular purchase decreases the likelihood of these motives.[28]

The model does not address one justification for RBPs that is com-

---

26. This multiproduct aspect could still be important if stores specialize in different types of music or videos. This seems more plausible in music markets than video rentals.

27. In at least one California and one Michigan city, cappuccino stands offer a free cup after purchase of a certain number previously. In both cities, the retail cappuccino market seems highly competitive, though the level of product differentiation is a point of frequent contention.

28. These programs could allow effective price discrimination if repeat buyers are "locals" who are more price sensitive or have lower search costs, while others are transient buyers who are less likely to shop around.

monly heard, but not generally credible. It is argued that economies of scale in production may justify RBPs on a cost basis. This is not the case, for two reasons. First, and most important, a single buyer's purchases are unlikely to have more than a trivial effect on marginal cost. Second, the economies are generally thought to be in production during a given period of time, while RBPs are usually time insensitive, except for the present value loss of delayed bonuses. For the scale economies argument to be applicable, a single buyer would have to comprise a nontrivial share of sales, the firm would have to have declining marginal cost— a stronger condition than simple scale economies—and the purchases would have to occur during a time period over which increased purchases cause decreased marginal cost.

Of course, one cannot rule out the effectiveness of these RBPs due to consumer myopia or irrationality. Consumers might systematically overestimate the probability that they will complete the number of purchases necessary to receive the bonus, or underestimate the time in which they will do so. The firm may have better information than consumers about these parameters, on average, so if consumer estimates are biased in the appropriate direction, the plans could yield positive profits, at least until consumer information improves. More generally, consumers may place value on the "gift" that exceeds the actual expected retail value. According to Fox 1968, there are extensive sociological studies of the place of gifts in commerce and trade dating back hundreds of years, though it is difficult to imagine that this effect would be very strong in these impersonal businesses and among the jaded customers in these markets.

One of a Set with Every Visit

Slightly more complex are RBPs that give away, or sell at steeply discounted prices, one of a set of a product—such as glasses, dishes, cookware, steak knives, or encyclopedias—with each purchase over time. Presumably these goods are more valuable when owned in sets, so the consumer has an incentive to return until he has collected a large number of the items. Gas stations have given away one tumbler or steak knife with each fill-up, while some supermarkets offer a different volume of an encyclopedia each month that can be purchased at discounted price with a minimum purchase of groceries.

These programs have two important features that distinguish them from those in the previous subsection. First, the bonus item is usually not manufactured or sold by the firm. Second, no accumulation of purchases over time is required to receive the bonus. Instead, the bonus item itself takes on greater value if more of them are acquired by the customer. These are goods that are normally owned in sets.

The attraction of using a bonus that the firm does not offer for sale is that giving the bonus is less likely to crowd out sales of the bonus item. The problem with this approach, as highlighted in the model, is that consumers are also more likely to value the bonus less than its production cost or the firm's acquisition cost. This seems more likely to be the case if the bonus item is low-quality steak knives or tumblers, which are available in highly competitive markets in which most scale economies are exhausted, than if it is encyclopedias, which are sold at great markups over marginal cost.

In fact, encyclopedias possess an ideal attribute of a bonus item. There are many potential consumers who value them at greater than marginal cost, but at less than the market price. The number of people who would buy a given brand of encyclopedia at even a discounted retail price is quite small, so the opportunity cost of most bonus uses is the printing cost of the encyclopedia, not the retail revenue forgone.

The drawback is that even the printing cost is substantial, so giving such a bonus to someone who places no value on it is a costly error. For this reason, supermarkets sell the encyclopedias at what is probably about marginal production cost—six dollars per volume in the case we observed—rather than offering them free of charge with a given size purchase. Dishes and cookware are also offered at about marginal cost by supermarkets on a similar time-limited basis for each piece of the set.

Trading Stamps

Trading stamps were one of the first examples of multi-outlet RBPs, in which points are earned through purchases in multiple locations and products of many different firms are available as bonuses. Trading stamps enjoyed periods of success in the early 1900s and again in the 1950s and 1960s, but have since virtually disappeared. The trading-stamp industry is not entirely deceased, but the reports of its death are not greatly exaggerated. The basic structure of the industry was that trading-stamp companies sold stamps to retailers, who then gave them away with retail sales. A given stamp company would generally sell to only one brand of each type of retail outlet in an area (for example, if the local Kroger grocery stores gave away S&H green stamps, then the A&P would not be allowed to buy the stamps from S&H). The stamps were collected by consumers and used to purchase goods at the trading-stamp company's redemption center.

Fox 1968 indicates that the stamps were sold to retailers at below their redemption value, valuing the bonus goods at normal retail prices. He quotes the CEO of Sperry & Hutchinson Company, the largest trading stamp company in the 1950s and 1960s, as claiming that the average consumer merchandise value was $1.16 for every $1 of stamp cost to the merchant.

This apparent expected gain for consumers was offset to some extent in two ways. First, some of the stamps were never redeemed, lowering the expected liability of the trading-stamp company. According to Fox, however, redemption rates for all of the major stamp companies were over 90 percent.[29] Second, the time between purchase of the stamps by retailers and redemption of them by consumers was significant, six to nine months on average, so the trading stamp company earned—and consumers lost—some return on the float. Still, if the S&H number is accurate, the stamps had slightly positive net value after accounting for redemption rates and lag time. If one recognizes in addition that this alternative currency required significant time in collecting stamps and pasting them into books and was much less liquid than cash—being redeemable at no more than one or two stores in a city and for only a limited range of goods—then it appears that the stamps offered little net value to consumers.[30]

Thus, it is likely that the merchant offering trading stamps was giving the consumer a gift that was valued less by the consumer than the cost of supplying the gift. The model in the previous section showed that the RBP is less likely to effectively deter entry or afford a competitive advantage against other firms when this is the case. At best, the consumer value was only a few percent greater than the merchant cost of the gift. This is a far cry from encyclopedia distributions or frequent-flier programs.

Nonetheless, for a period of more than a decade in the 1950s and early 1960s, trading stamps were extremely popular. Over 80 percent of U.S. households reported that they collected trading stamps.[31] Supermarkets

---

29. It has been argued that trading stamps were a means of price discriminating between collectors and noncollectors. With an over 90 percent redemption rate, this is a poor discriminatory technique, unless merchants simply didn't distribute the stamps to the consumers that it knew or thought to be noncollectors. Furthermore, even if the redemption rate was only 50 percent, the merchant's discriminatory gains would be costly, because the rate it paid for the stamps was independent of how many of the stamps it distributed were actually redeemed. Stamps thrown away cost the merchant just as much as stamps redeemed.

30. Finally, it is worth recognizing that the trading-stamp companies had no incentive to bias downward the estimated redemption value of their stamps and a good reason to bias the figure upward.

31. Fox 1968, 19.

that did not have the local franchise of the most popular stamp felt at a significant disadvantage. Managers of competing firms reported that price discounting was ineffective in their attempts to offset the attraction of the firms that distributed the most popular brand of stamps.[32] Thus, for some period at least, trading stamps seemed to give substantial competitive advantage against other incumbents. Why were trading stamps so effective for a period of time and why did they so rapidly lose their importance in competition and marketing?

It has been argued by Fox and others that trading stamps lost their effectiveness as women reentered the workforce in greater numbers at the end of the baby boom. As the value of these former homemakers' time increased, the nuisance cost of collecting and redeeming stamps did the same. But, as shown above, even with zero nuisance cost, stamps did not offer much, if any, net value. The social or cultural trend of trading stamps may have caught the fancy of many people or it may simply have taken consumers some time to recognize the true redemption value of the stamps.

Trading stamps were also in some ways the precursors to the discount buying clubs that are now popular. Trading-stamp catalogs offered one style of most items and purchased those items in large quantities from the manufacturers. The limited selection and the low-service redemption centers—few items were on display for closer examination before purchase—gave the impression of discount retailing. Perhaps consumers were misled by these appearances for some time.

Incentive conflicts within the traditional family might also have contributed to the success of trading stamps when the traditional family structure was at its apex. The homemaking wife wanted to spend a higher proportion of family income on household goods—particularly labor-saving appliances—than did the working husband, who did fewer of the household chores and spent less time in the home. While direct purchases of these items could be monitored easily, it was more difficult for the husband to dispute that the shopping wife was getting the trading stamp as a bonus, while still buying groceries and other goods at the lowest prices available. In fact, the majority of the bonus items offered by stamp companies were household goods. Table 1 shows the breakdown of merchandise delivered by the 10 largest stamp companies during 1966. Soft goods (e.g., sheets, tablecloths), housewares (e.g., pots and pans), furniture, and appliances together account for nearly half of the merchandise value. Thus, the success of trading stamps may have stemmed in part from an intrahousehold principal/agent problem. As

---

32. See Fox 1968, 37.

TABLE 1.   Merchandise Distributed by Trading-Stamp Companies in 1966

Soft goods	16.7%	Bathroom accessories	3.6%
Housewares	11.4%	Clocks	3.2%
Furniture	10.2%	Luggage	2.5%
Appliances	9.2%	Glasses and dishes	2.3%
Toys	6.3%	Radios	2.3%
Jewelry and personal	5.5%	Tools	2.2%
Gift Items	4.6%	Lawn supplies	1.8%
Juvenile	4.4%	Silver and flatware	1.5%
Sporting goods	4.3%	Cameras	1.3%
Outdoor accessories	3.9%	Books	0.8%
		Miscellaneous	2.0%

Source: Data from Fox 1968, 98.

women returned to the labor force this conflict of preferences and incentives diminished.

Airline Frequent-Flier Programs

Airline FFPs are probably the most successful of the modern RBPs, because they combine nearly all of the attributes for an effective RBP. When sufficiently restricted, the bonuses offered in FFPs have very low marginal cost to airlines. They are trips or upgrades to first class that occupy seats that would otherwise be empty. The most significant way in which these trips are costly to the airline is that they potentially replace a trip for which the consumer would otherwise pay. The sophistication of airline price discrimination through yield management means that fewer trips valued at above marginal cost are left unsold. Still, marginal cost can be quite low if availability is restricted and most airlines now place substantially tighter restrictions on the use of FFP bonus trips than on the most deeply discounted tickets. Thus, many FFP bonus trips would not have occurred otherwise.

   In the airline industry, probably more than in any other, the companies have been able to exploit the principal/agent separation in use of the RBP.[33] As pointed out in the model, the principal/agent separation raises the agent's shadow value of the bonus unit, V, and thus makes the RBP more effective. This additional private value of the V unit as a

---

   33. Since the focus here is retail RBPs, I do not discuss here the use of travel agent commission override programs (TACOs) used by airlines to encourage travel agents to book more traffic on their flights. These programs, which operate much like RBPs but usually pay cash bonuses, may be more important than FFPs in influencing successful airline marketing. See Borenstein 1992 for a discussion of TACOs.

bonus is lost if the bonus unit is sold directly to the agent, since few workers could or would engage in the fraud necessary to purchase a personal airline ticket with the employer's money.

The airline industry also offers natural groupings of customers according to their preferred products that facilitate the use of an RBP to one firm's competitive advantage. A customer who lives in Pittsburgh is much more interested in the range of flights from Pittsburgh on which she can earn FFP points in a given airline's plan than the selection of flights from Detroit. Similarly, the Pittsburgh resident's value of the FFP bonus will be directly related to the number of destinations easily reached from Pittsburgh that are in the set of bonuses offered. An airline with significantly more service at Pittsburgh than others will have an advantage in offering an attractive set of products on which to earn RBP points and an attractive range of goods on which the bonuses can be spent. Thus, the hub and network production economies in airlines significantly augment the use of the FFP, because it corresponds to a dominant share of the air-travel services that a person living near the hub is likely to purchase.

To see the importance of this localized market dominance, consider the effectiveness of an RBP in an industry where consumers desire many different products that are manufactured in the industry, but where there is no correlation of consumers' demand across products. Scale and scope economies in production are likely to be exhausted at a much smaller level of output relative to total market output in the entire industry than in any smaller localized market. Thus, company shares for the industry as a whole are likely to be more nearly equal than shares in sales of individual products. The option value of a bonus on a firm that produces 40 percent of the products in the industry product line is likely to be little larger than the option value of a bonus on a firm that produces 30 percent of the industry products if the preferences over products preferred for bonus consumption are distributed randomly. More to the point, if all firms produce virtually all products in the industry, then RBPs are unlikely to produce a competitive advantage for one firm over others in any of the markets.

Air travel has so many attractive attributes as an RBP bonus that many companies in other industries have made arrangements to offer air travel as a bonus through an existing airline FFP. Institutionally, the company pays the airline for FFP points that it then gives away to customers. The price at which this transaction occurs varies, but is generally below one cent per FFP point distributed. This is presumably at least the airline's marginal cost of this liability, but probably below the value that some consumers get from receiving the mileage.[34]

The attraction of airline travel, as well as hotel services, as an RBP bonus is clear for companies that want to operate an RBP but only produce goods that sell for close to marginal cost. Theoretically, the arrangement between the airline and the other company could be structured so that the FFP miles are purchased at marginal cost and, possibly, a lump-sum fee is paid in order to allocate the rents from this use of FFP miles. In fact, however, airlines are generally compensated on a more nearly linear basis, and the price seems to be above marginal cost. Recognizing this along with the fact that nontrivial coordination and transaction costs exist in these arrangements,[35] it is surprising that FFP miles remain such a popular bonus for other RBPs.

Credit Card RBPs

While trading stamps have virtually vanished, bonuses on credit card purchases that have some of the same attributes have recently appeared. Some credit card companies offer bonuses of a selection of household goods at zero or discounted price. Other credit cards give mileage on airline FFPs as the bonus. A few companies, including Discover credit card, offer *cash* rebates on credit card purchases. Most recently, major production companies, such as General Motors, have begun to offer MasterCard or Visa credit cards that allow the buyer to earn discounts on the goods the company makes, autos in the case of General Motors.

Issuers of all cards that use RBPs do so to entice consumers to carry, and make purchases with, one card over others or over other forms of payments. The issuers of proprietary cards—Discover, American Express, or Diners Club—do so also to expand acceptance of the cards by merchants who find an increasing number of customers asking to use the card.[36] The RBPs range from virtually valueless—with Citibank *Citidollars* you can earn the right to purchase certain goods at

---

34. This information is based on discussions with one former and one current executive at major U.S. airlines. Even at one cent per FFP point, the 20,000 points necessary to earn a free domestic round trip on most airlines cost only $200, below the cost of most supersaver discount trips.

35. Levine 1987 discusses the coordination costs of cooperative frequent-flier programs with many participating airlines.

36. This is less likely to be an incentive for issuers of MasterCard or Visa, because acceptance of these cards is independent of which affiliate of these consortiums is the issuer, but the RBP policy varies for each MC- or Visa-affiliated card.

prices that are not noticeably below those of major discount stores—to clearly worth a significant dollar equivalent.

Nearly all of these programs offer increasing marginal payments; for example, the percentage of total charges paid back in cash by Discover increases with the total amount charged over the year. While the relationship between quantity of miles awarded and total charges is linear on the FFP-related credit cards, the bonuses available for FFP miles from airlines generally increase nonlinearly with mileage accumulated, as discussed earlier. The nonlinear bonus schedules combined with the annual fee, which can be $75 or more, create the incentive for a person to carry and use only one general-use credit card.

A primary problem with most of these programs is the same as with trading stamps: except for the recent entrants, credit card companies have no particular advantage in producing, acquiring, or distributing the goods or services that are the bonuses. The value of the bonus to the consumer is unlikely to be much greater than the cost to the credit card company of supplying the bonus. This is obvious with the credit card RBPs that simply give away cash according to a nonlinear schedule. There may be some gain in the distribution of airline FFP points as a bonus for using the credit card, but it is likely to be much smaller than when airlines use their own product as the RBP bonus. The auto and other good-producing companies that have recently entered the credit card market are offering discounts on the goods they produce as bonuses. This has the potential to be an effective and successful approach, since autos generally sell at significant retail markups, but will depend on how many of the resulting car sales would have occurred even without the credit card program.

Credit card RBPs are inferior to trading stamps and airline FFPs because the network structures of the competing companies are virtually identical. Credit card acceptance is homogeneous for all Visa and MasterCard affiliated cards. Unlike the regional specialization of airlines or the cross-product specialization of trading stamps, one credit card offers pretty much the same array of services as another. This is less true for the proprietary cards, which have less general acceptance, but may have services that the Visa and MasterCard affiliates do not offer. Still, the vast majority of the uses for even Discover and American Express overlap with the uses for Visa and MasterCard.

How, then, have credit card RBPs been as successful as they have? One reason may be the noneconomic behavior that people seem to exhibit with respect to credit card choice and use, as documented by Ausubel 1991. Competition on the terms of the cards—interest rate, grace period, free insurance coverage, and so on—seems to be fairly ineffective, so credit card companies have turned to alternative forms of competition, such as RBPs. This may even explain the use of cash bonuses if the trade-off between the cost of the service (i.e., interest rate and annual fee) and the cost of the bonus is not fully understood by the consumer.

Credit card RBPs also benefit from a more subtle principal/agent problem. Many merchants that take credit cards would still prefer cash payment in order to avoid the credit card fee they are charged, which can be as high as 5 percent. When a person decides to use a credit card due to its RBP, rather than pay cash, the merchant loses revenue. It is almost certainly the case that the merchant fee is above the marginal cost of the transaction, so the bonus from using the card more frequently is paid in part by card company profits from additional merchant fees.

Long-Distance Telephone

With the breakup of AT&T, the entry of competing long-distance carriers, and the partial deregulation of long-distance telephone rates, long-distance telephone service became a much more competitive market in the early 1980s. By the end of the decade, the two largest entrants into the long-distance market, MCI and Sprint, had begun to use RBPs in their marketing. MCI has hooked up with two airlines to offer FFP points with every phone call. Sprint began an RBP that offers bonuses that include free long-distance calls, free air travel and hotel stays, and some free consumer goods. AT&T joined *Air Miles*, an RBP that was operated jointly by food companies, hotels, a car company, and others, in which purchase of any good earns points toward free air travel. The program ceased U.S. operation in May of 1993, however.

The major long-distance (LD) phone companies all offer virtually complete coverage of the long-distance product market. Unlike firms in the airline industry, none of the major LD carriers has a regional advantage or otherwise offers a significantly wider array of products that would make one more attractive to a class of consumers than the other carriers. Furthermore, as a result of the virtually complete geographic coverage by each company and the "one plus" dialing technology, few consumers use multiple LD carriers. The most significant competition occurs at the point that an LD carrier is chosen.

Due to the necessity of broad geographic coverage by an LD carrier, these RBPs probably do not give one carrier a competitive advantage over others. The nonlinear aspect of the payoff schedules is unlikely to present a permanent competitive advantage as it did in the model when one firm served more markets than the other. Of course, the nonlinear payoff can still deter switching of attached customers in the short run, as it does with even the more primitive RBPs discussed above, and could present a barrier to entry.

The LD carriers have not developed particularly good bonuses for their RBPs either. The Sprint program, *Callers' Plus*, offers free travel, merchandise, or long-distance calling. With the first two of these, the firm is purchasing these products. As with trading stamps, there is no clear reason why LD companies would be particularly efficient distributors of these products or able to buy them at lower prices than other bulk marketers. With free phone calls, the firm is almost certainly crowding out sale of units that would otherwise be paid for. If the two hours of free calls that are available for a relatively low number of collected points are simply deducted from the monthly bill then the bonus is simply the cash equivalent. More effective, it seems, would be free calling during a prespecified period of a certain evening or a day. That would probably displace fewer calls that would otherwise be paid for.

Thus, LD telephone companies do not seem particularly well positioned to use the RBPs discussed so far as a competitive weapon, despite the network configuration of demand and production. As discussed above and shown in the model, a *comparatively* wider variety of products that are of interest to a customer make the RBP more effective. Had they been allowed to, AT&T could probably have used an RBP quite successfully in the early 1980s when its competitors offered connections to only a limited set of domestic cities. Now that all LD carriers effectively have complete service, the long-run competitive advantage of offering an RBP has diminished.

MCI, however, has taken a different approach with its *Friends and Family* program. This program gives a discount on connections to frequently called numbers and makes that discount much larger if the number called is also a subscriber to the same LD company. Sprint's program, *The Most*, has mimicked many aspects of the MCI plan. Where airlines have been able to take advantage of locational dominance to target customers of similar demand patterns, MCI found a way to use the two-party nature of telephone consumption to accomplish a similar goal. Rather than giving a bonus to a single repeat buyer to get her to stay with one company over time, the program gives a bonus (actually calling discounts) to groups of buyers, creating an incentive for each buyer to make sure that all others in the group buy from the same company.

Once established, the program offers much the same long-run advantage that an FFP offers an airline in the area where it dominates service. The dominance of service is not regional in this case, but "route specific," where the routes are the connections to another specific set of telephone numbers. The cost of switching can be enormous once a person has joined such a plan, since many others in his or her telephone community will have subscribed to the same system and one person switching has significant pecuniary externalities. Due to the high coordination cost of switching, the MCI program could lock in customers quite effectively. The basis for the consumer loyalty is attachment, not in the temporal sense of the RBPs discussed above, but in a community sense where economies of coordination across individuals have been created by the program.

The weakness in this analogy appears to be that the bonus given in these programs is not goods, but cash discounts on calls. Even here a parallel exists, however. The pricing analog to offering bonuses that are valued above marginal cost but don't crowd out sales is offering discounts on units for which demand is particularly price-elastic while maintaining price well above marginal cost for other units. The *Friends and Family* type of program provides discounts targeted at particular types of calls—calls to one's most frequently contacted friends and family—which, in all likelihood, are more price-elastic than other long-distance calls.

Conclusion

This essay has demonstrated that even the most simple repeat-buyer programs can have some effect in deterring entry by inducing short-run customer loyalty. The more effective RBPs can also afford one firm a long-run competitive advantage over new entrants and existing rivals. The long-run advantage, however, is critically dependent on the firm's ability to offer a bonus that is valued more highly by the buyer than it costs the firm to provide, including the opportunity cost due to forgone sale of the bonus item. The ideal bonus product would be one that is generally sold for a price well above marginal cost and for which there is a large set of people who value the good at more than marginal cost, but at less than the price, and who cannot be effectively captured through price discrimination.

The principal/agent problem inherent in those RBPs that give personal bonuses to people making purchases for a company greatly enhances the effectiveness of the RBP. These buyers are likely to value the bonus more than the shadow value of additional dollars spent to acquire the RBP bonus. Thus, in these cases, the RBP becomes a kickback to purchasing agents. This probably explains the greater success of airline FFPs than RBPs in industries that primarily sell products for personal use.

If the firm can use the RBP to distribute items that are valued above (opportunity) cost without exploiting a principal/agent separation, then the RBP is essentially a form of price discrimination. Like price discrimination, the RBP can increase or decrease welfare. If success of the program relies on the principal/agent problem, then the RBP is much more likely to diminish social welfare.

If those elements necessary for establishing a long-run advantage with an RBP are present, then the degree of loyalty inducement from a given type of consumer will increase if the program allows points to be earned on a wide variety of products that these consumers buy, particularly if it offers a wider variety of products than competing RBPs. The effective RBP encourages a consumer to concentrate purchases of a type of goods with just one company. The most attractive company will be the one that offers a wide variety of goods. Similarly, the program that allows a wide variety of bonus products that appeal to a consumer will be more successful, because the variety of bonus products directly affects the expected value of collecting points in the program.

Finally, it would be a mistake to discount the possible role of consumer myopia and misunderstanding in the success of RBPs. Firms are likely to have better information about the true probabilities of achieving the bonus, and are likely to present the program in a way that leads consumers to overestimate these probabilities. Perhaps consumers are not easily fooled, or perhaps they learn the truth relatively quickly, but it is likely that misperceptions are a nontrivial factor affecting RBP effectiveness.

The airline industry is probably best suited to make profitable use of RBPs because it offers the network economies and network differentiation that augment the program while also effectively exploiting principal/agent separation. While the trading-stamp industry took advantage of similar network affiliation effects, it suffered from a general dearth of good bonus offerings, and was only able to exploit an intrafamily principal/agent problem that was probably much weaker than that the airlines have tapped. Credit card RBPs are still more difficult to explain, given the commonality in network coverage, a similar shortage of good bonus items, and an even weaker principal/agent problem. Though credit card companies could potentially compete more efficiently on interest rates and other fees, it seems that consumers are nearly oblivious when it comes to credit card fees and interest rates. RBPs might emerge by default as the focus of competition.

Attempts by long-distance telephone companies to adopt a traditional RBP seem to have been relatively unsuccessful, probably due again to the great overlap in product coverage among the major competitors and their inability to exploit a principal/agent problem. The MCI innovation of the RBP-like *Friends and Family* program has been more successful, because the program creates network coverage differentiation. Furthermore, the social costs of switching once an individual is attached can be large because of the pecuniary externality the program creates. The payoff to these programs are discounts on the primary product sold, which does not seem to be the ideal bonus. Calling discounts could be quite successful rewards if the calls associated with the program are much more price-elastic than other residential long-distance calls.

Telecommunications more generally seems to offer many possibilities for strategic use of RBPs. Prices of many products are well above marginal cost, price discrimination can be very difficult due to institutional and regulatory constraints, and most telecommunication firms offer a variety of products that differ in their appeal to different classes of customers. As the links between different forms of telecommunication increase, the possibilities for RBP use will multiply. Recent discussions between long-distance phone companies and cable television operators could lead to RBPs that reward local users of a company's long-distance service with free access to cable channels that are otherwise priced well above the operator's marginal cost. Such an offer could improve the economic efficiency of cable television distribution, but could have anticompetitive effects on the long-distance market. Similarly, companies that operate both local cellular phone services and long-distance companies could use the local dominance in one market to profitably differentiate their RBPs. The sophistication with which these programs are used has greatly increased in the last 10 years. Refinement will surely continue through the 1990s.

REFERENCES

Adams, W. James, and Janet Yellen. 1976. "Commodity Bundling and the Burden of Monopoly." *Quarterly Journal of Economics* (August).

Ausubel, Lawrence M. 1991. "The Failure of Competition in the Credit Card Market." *American Economic Review* 81 (March).

Banerjee, Abhijit, and Lawrence Summers. 1987. "On Frequent-Flyer Programs and Other Loyalty-Inducing Economic Arrangements." Cambridge, MA: Harvard Institute of Economic Research Discussion Paper #1337, September.

Borenstein, Severin. 1989. "Hubs and High Fares: Airport Dominance and Market Power in the U.S. Airline Industry." *Rand Journal of Economics* 20 (Autumn).

Borenstein, Severin. 1991. "The Dominant-Firm Advantage in Multi-Product Industries: Evidence from the U.S. Airlines." *Quarterly Journal of Economics* 106 (November).

Borenstein, Severin. 1992. "The Evolution of U.S. Airline Competition." *Journal of Economic Perspectives* 7 (Spring).

Cairns, Robert D., and John W. Galbraith. 1990. "Artificial Compatibility, Barriers to Entry, and Frequent-Flyer Programs." *Canadian Journal of Economics* 23, no. 4 (November).

Caminal, Ramon, and Carmen Matutes. 1990. "Endogenous Switching Costs in a Duopoly Model." *International Journal of Industrial Organization* 8 (September).

Carnevale, Mary Lu. 1992. "AT&T-McCaw Link Stuns Baby Bells." *Wall Street Journal*, November 6.

Carnevale, Mary Lu. 1993. "Ameritech Wants to Enter Long Distance." *Wall Street Journal*, February 23.

Fox, Harold W. 1968. *The Economics of Trading Stamps.* Washington, D.C.: Public Affairs Press.

French, Trevor. 1991. "Better By Miles?" *Airline Business,* October.

Keller, John J., and Mark Robichaux. 1993. "MCI Talks to Entertainment Firm, Cable TV Concerns about Partnerships." *Wall Street Journal*, March 30.

Klemperer, Paul. 1987a. "The Competitiveness of Markets with Consumer Switching Costs." *Rand Journal of Economics* 18 (Spring).

Klemperer, Paul. 1987b. "Entry Deterrence in Markets with Consumer Switching Costs." *Economic Journal* 8.

Levine, Michael E. 1987. "Airline Competition in Deregulated Markets: Theory, Firm Strategy, and Public Policy." *Yale Journal on Regulation* 4 (Spring).

Roberts, Johnnie L., and Mark Robichaux. 1993. "Time Warner, US West Said To Be in Talks." *Wall Street Journal,* March 15.

Roberts, Johnnie L., and Mary Lu Carnevale. 1993. "Time Warner Plans Electronic 'Superhighway.' " *Wall Street Journal*, January 27.

U.S. Department of Transportation. 1990. *Secretary's Task Force on Competition in the U.S. Domestic Airline Industry.* Washington, D.C.: U.S. Government Printing Office.

Contributors

Donald L. Alexander is associate professor of economics at Western Michigan University. He earned his Ph.D. in economics from Penn State University. Before joining WMU, he held faculty positions at the College of William and Mary and Penn State University and professional positions at the Federal Trade Commission, Capital Economics (a consulting firm), and the International Trade Commission. He has published articles in the areas of industrial organization, antitrust economics, and regulation in professional journals such as the *Southern Economic Journal, Applied Economics, Review of Industrial Organization,* and *Economics Letters.* In addition, he has an article forthcoming in the American Enterprise Institute's *Competitive Strategies in the U.S. Pharmaceutical Industry.* He has been the recipient of the Philip S. McKenna Fellowship for the Study of Market Economics and has served as a consultant to Michigan Bell and the Upjohn Company.

Severin Borenstein is associate professor of economics and director of the University of California Program on Workable Energy Regulation at the University of California, Davis. He has taught at the University of Michigan, Berkeley's Haas School of Business, and Stanford University's Graduate School of Business. Prior to his academic career, Borenstein was a staff economist at the U.S. Civil Aeronautics Board. He is also a research associate of the National Bureau of Economic Research and of the Institute of Governmental Affairs and Institute of Transportation Studies at U.C. Davis. Borenstein received his Ph.D. in economics from MIT. He has written extensively on competition in the airline, oil, and gasoline industries. His studies of the airline industry, which focused attention on the competitive advantage and market power that results when an airline dominates an airport, are considered very influential in the formation of U.S. airline policy since 1987. His work has appeared in *American Economic Review, Rand Journal of Economics, Quarterly Journal of Economics, Journal of Regulatory Economics,* and other scholarly journals. Borenstein has advised airlines, oil companies, computer maintenance companies, insurance companies, and state and federal agencies on antitrust and regulation issues.

Kenneth D. Boyer is professor of economics at Michigan State University. He has held visiting positions at FuDan University in Shanghai, the International Institute of Management in Berlin, and the University of Michigan in Ann Arbor. He earned his Ph.D. in economics from the University of Michigan. Boyer is an industrial organization economist who has a keen interest in regulation of transportation industries. He is a member of the editorial board of the *Review of Industrial Organization* and a member of the Committee for the Study of Public Policy for Surface Freight Transportation for the Transportation Research Board of the National Academy of Sciences. He is frequently called upon to referee submitted articles to top-level economics journals. Boyer has published over thirty scholarly articles in books and in journals such as the *American Economic Review*, the *Journal of Political Economy, Review of Economics and Statistics, Rand Journal of Economics, Southern Economic Journal*, and the *Review of Industrial Organization*.

Richard J. Gilbert is professor of economics and professor of business administration at the University of California, Berkeley. For the past decade he has also served as director of the University of California Energy Research Institute. In addition, he is a principal and member of the Board of Directors of Law and Economics Consulting Group. At the time of writing Gilbert is on leave serving as deputy assistant attorney general, U.S. Department of Justice. He earned his Ph.D. in engineering-economic systems from Stanford University. He has published several books, the most recent being *The Environment of Oil* and *Regulatory Choices: A Perspective on Developments in Energy Policy*. His scholarly articles have appeared in the *American Economic Review, Rand Journal of Economics, Journal of Economic Theory, Review of Economic Studies, European Economic Review,* and the *Journal of Industrial Economics*. Gilbert is the associate editor of three journals, has been on National Science Foundation review panels, has been an advisor to the U.S. Department of Energy, and is a member of the Advisory Board of the California Institute for Energy Efficiency and the Electric Power Research Institute.

James L. Hamilton is professor and chair of the Department of Finance and Business Economics at Wayne State University. He previously had taught and held an administrative post at Grinnell College. He earned his Ph.D. from Duke University. Hamilton is an industrial organization economist specializing in questions regarding vertical integration, competition, and the economics of stock markets. Hamilton has contributed chapters in books and written numerous scholarly articles. His work has appeared in the *Journal of Law and Economics, Review of Economics and Statistics, Journal of Financial and Quantitative Analysis, Journal of Finance, Southern Economic Journal,* and the *Review of Industrial Organization.* Hamilton is frequently called upon to appear as an expert witness and to referee submissions to professional journals.

Jerry A. Hausman is MacDonald Professor of Economics at the Massachusetts Institute of Technology, where he has taught for more than two decades. For most of that time he has also been research associate of the National Bureau of Economic Research. Hausman is director of the MIT Telecommunications Economics Research Program and on the Board of Directors of the Theseus Institute at the France Telecom University. He earned his Ph.D. from Oxford University. He is a fellow of the Econometric Society, has received the Frisch Medal from the Society, and has presented the Fisher-Schultz and Jacob Marschak Lectures for the Society. In 1985 Hausman received the John Bates Clark Award of the American Economic Association. He has been associate editor for several journals and still serves in that capacity for the *Journal of Public Economics* and the *Journal of Applied Econometrics.* Hausman has published widely in the fields of econometrics, public finance, and industrial organization and regulation. He has published several books, chapters in books, many reports, and a large number of scholarly articles in journals such as *Econometrica, Journal of Econometrics, Journal of Applied Econometrics, American Economic Review, Journal of Political Economy, Journal of Public Economics,* and *Rand Journal of Economics.*

Edward Kahn is scientist and leader, Utility Policy Planning Group in the Energy and Environment Division at Lawrence Berkeley Laboratory. He is also a lecturer in the Energy and Resources Program at the University of California, Berkeley, and holds the title of research economist in the University-wide Energy Research Group at Berkeley. Dr. Kahn is frequently called upon to consult for utilities, state agencies, and private companies. He has served as an expert witness before regulatory commissions in several states. He is the author of *Electric Utility Planning and Regulation,* now in its second edition. Kahn has published articles in a number of scholarly journals including the *Journal of Regulatory Economics, Journal of Political Economy, Public Utility Fortnightly, Energy Systems and Policy,* the *Electricity Journal, Energy Economics,* and *Energy: The International Journal.*

Jeffrey K. MacKie-Mason is associate professor of economics and public policy and associate research scientist, Institute of Public Policy Studies at the University of Michigan, Ann Arbor. He is also research associate of the National Bureau of Economic Research. He earned his Ph.D. at Massachusetts Institute of Technology. MacKie-Mason has been a national fellow at the Hoover Institution, Stanford University; a visiting faculty scholar at the University of Oslo in Norway; and a visiting scholar at the California Energy Institute, University of California, Berkeley. He is an active researcher in the fields of industrial organization/regulation and public finance. He has been the recipient of several grants and is presently doing research on two different NSF grants. He has contributed several chapters to scholarly books and conference volumes. His research articles have appeared in *Rand Journal of Economics, Journal of Public Economics,* the *Journal of Economic Perspectives, Quarterly Journal of Economics, Journal of Finance, Oxford Review of Economic Policy, Economics Letters,* and *Review of Economics and Statistics.* MacKie-Mason has served as a referee for NSF, Canadian SSRC, and about twenty top-level economics and finance journals.

Dennis Ray is assistant professor of business and codirector of the Wisconsin Public Utility Institute at the University of Wisconsin, Madison. Prior to joining the faculty at the University of Wisconsin, Ray was research analyst in the Chief Economist's Office of the Wisconsin Public Service Commission. He earned his M.B.A. in finance and Ph.D. in transportation and public utilities from the University of Wisconsin, Madison. Ray is vice-chair of the Transportation and Public Utilities Group of the American Economic Association. He has published numerous reports on such subjects as lifeline rates and the value of transmission security, as well as articles in professional journals such as the *Journal of Regulatory Economics, Utility Policy, Transactions on Power Systems, Journal of the American Planning Association,* and *Electric Potential.*

Lee L. Selwyn is president of Economics and Technology, Inc. (ETI). He is an internationally recognized authority on telecommunication economics, regulation, and public policy. As founder of ETI, Dr. Selwyn has formulated and developed numerous policy recommendations and regulatory devices that have been widely embraced by policy makers at all levels. He has provided expert testimony and analysis on technology, rate design, service cost analysis, market structure, form of regulation, and numerous other telecommunication policy issues before more than forty state commissions, the FCC, the United States Congress, the Canadian Radiotelevision and Telecommunications Commission, and the

British Office of Telecommunications. Dr. Selwyn has also appeared as a speaker on numerous panels around the world, and has published dozens of articles on telecommunication industry issues. He received his Ph.D. at the Alfred P. Sloan School of Management, Massachusetts Institute of Technology.

Werner Sichel is professor of economics and chair of the Department of Economics at Western Michigan University. His field of specialty is industrial organization. Sichel earned his Ph.D. from Northwestern University. He was a Fulbright-Hays senior lecturer at the University of Belgrade and a visiting scholar at the Hoover Institution, Stanford University. Sichel is a past president of the Economics Society of Michigan, the Midwest Business Economics Association, and is the current president of the Midwest Economics Association. For the past decade he has served as a consultant to a "baby bell" and to a major law firm. He serves on the Editorial Advisory Board of the *Antitrust Law and Economics Review* and *The Quarterly Review of Economics and Finance*. Sichel has published a number of articles in scholarly journals and books and is the author or editor of seventeen books. His books include several principles texts, *Economics*, and *Basic Economic Concepts*; and a reference book, *Economics Journals and Serials: An Analytical Guide*; three edited books in the field of industrial organization, *Industrial Organization and Public Policy, Antitrust Policy and Economic Welfare*, and *The Economic Effects of Multinational Corporations;* five edited books in the area of public utility regulation; and edited books containing essays by past members of the Council of Economic Advisers and Nobel Laureates.

Rodney Stevenson is professor of business and executive director of the Wisconsin Public Utility Institute at the University of Wisconsin, Madison. He is also a member of the faculty of the university's Institute for Environmental Studies and chair of its Energy Analysis and Policy Program. Prior to his present position, he was a member of the economics faculty of Michigan State University and the University of Maryland and held posts with the U.S. Federal Power Commission and the U.S. Postal Rate Commission. Stevenson earned his Ph.D. from Michigan State University. Stevenson has served as a consultant, advisor, and expert witness for numerous state, federal, and international governmental organizations; for public utility firms; and for consumer and environmental organizations. His research interests have focused on regulatory economics and policy, institutional economics, and performance measurement. He has published numerous books and reports, as well as articles in scholarly journals including the *American Economic Review, Journal of Economet-*

rics, Columbia Journal of World Business, International Economic Review, Journal of Economic Issues, Land Economics, Journal of Economics and Business, and *Public Utilities Fortnightly.*

Harry M. Trebing is Emeritus Professor of Economics at Michigan State University and senior fellow of the MSU Institute of Public Utilities, the institute he directed for twenty-five years. He is also adjunct professor at both Michigan State University and New Mexico State University. Prior to coming to MSU, Trebing taught at the University of Nebraska and Indiana University. He earned his Ph.D. from the University of Wisconsin, Madison. For many years Trebing served as administrator of the education programs of the National Association of Regulatory Utility Commissioners and as a public member of the board of the National Regulatory Research Institute. He is a member of the editorial boards of two professional journals. As the editor of numerous publications, he writes and lectures extensively in the fields of energy and telecommunications. Trebing is a past chairman of the Transportation and Public Utilities Group of the American Economic Association, a past president of the Association for Evolutionary Economics, and a past member of various government advisory panels, including the Congressional Office of Technology Assessment, the U.S. General Accounting Office, the National Science Foundation, and the National Research Council. He served as chief economist with the Federal Communications Commission and the U.S. Postal Rate Commission.

Hal R. Varian is Reuben Kempf Professor of Economics and professor of finance at the University of Michigan, Ann Arbor. Before coming to Michigan he taught at MIT. He earned his Ph.D. from the University of California, Berkeley. He has been a visiting professor at Arizona, Berkeley, Stanford, Stockholm, Helsinki, Oxford, and Monash in Australia. Varian has received many honors and awards, including being an NSF Fellow, a Gugenheim Fellow, an Erskine Fellow, and a fellow of the Econometrics Society. He was coeditor of the *American Economic Review* and is now an associate editor. He also serves on eight other editorial boards of journals. Varian is the author of several books including the best-selling and much translated *Microeconomic Analysis* and *Intermediate Microeconomics* (both in their third edition). He has also contributed many chapters to scholarly books and has published widely in top-level economics journals, including several each in the *Journal of Public Economics, Econometrica, Journal of Economic Theory, American Economic Review, Journal of Econometrics, Economic Inquiry,* and *Scandinavian Journal of Economics.*

Matthew White is assistant professor of economics at the Graduate School of Business, Stanford University. He specializes in econometrics, statistics, industrial organization, and regulation. He has assisted in studies of wholesale power markets, power pooling, and transmission access policy and has analyzed cost and performance data for the U.S. electric utility industry at the University of California Energy Institute (Berkeley). White has also assisted in the development of a long-term energy forecasting model for the U.S. Department of Energy and has analyzed the structure of major energy markets and the behavior of energy producers for the Engineering Research Division of the Systems Research Group at Lawrence Livermore National Laboratory.